I am impressed with how the authors
have taken major issues of dysfunction and
shared them in an insightful, practical
and easy-to-understand way.
This personally honest book
is written in such a way that readers
can identify easily with the authors.
It will help them deal with important
issues — and it will hold their attention.

Dr. H. Norman Wright, Director
Christian Marriage Enrichment

The Franks give tender new hope
and encouragement to couples
who have experienced victimization —
and to those who minister in this area.
WHEN VICTIMS MARRY drafts
a beautiful picture of the healing process.
The authors' analogy to building a home
provides steps to wholeness
and godly incentives for couples
to face truth. As a result,
wounded marriages can be drawn
into His healing light.

Lana Bateman, founder of
Philippian Ministries, Inc.
and author of
GOD'S CRIPPLED CHILDREN

Jan Frank is also the author of

Door of Hope

published by
Here's Life Publishers

When VICTIMS MARRY

by *Don and Jan Frank*

Here's Life Publishers

First Printing, February 1990
Second Printing, April 1990

Published by
HERE'S LIFE PUBLISHERS, INC.
P. O. Box 1576
San Bernardino, CA 92402

Library of Congress Cataloging-in-Publication Data
   Frank, Don.
         When victims marry : building a stronger marriage by
      breaking destructive cycles / Don and Jan Frank.

            p.   cm.

         ISBN 0-89840-274-3

         1. Marriage — Religious aspects — Christianity.   I. Frank,
      Jan.   II. Title.
      BV835.F72   1990
      248.8'44 — dc20   89-26984
                                                             CIP

Unless otherwise indicated, Scripture references are taken from the New King
James Version of the Bible. Other versions used are: The Amplified Bible (AMP),
the New American Standard Bible (NASB), the New International Version (NIV),
and the King James Version (KJV).

For More Information, Write:
L.I.F.E. — P.O. Box A399, Sydney South 2000, Australia
Campus Crusade for Christ of Canada — Box 300, Vancouver, B.C., V6C 2X3, Canada
Campus Crusade for Christ — Pearl Assurance House, 4 Temple Row, Birmingham, B2 5HG, England
Lay Institute for Evangelism — P.O. Box 8786, Auckland 3, New Zealand
Campus Crusade for Christ — P.O. Box 240, Raffles City Post Office, Singapore 9117
Great Commission Movement of Nigeria — P.O. Box 500, Jos, Plateau State Nigeria, West Africa
Campus Crusade for Christ International — Arrowhead Springs, San Bernardino, CA 92414, U.S.A.

With deepest affection, we dedicate
this book
to our two daughters,
Heather and Kellie.
We are "friends forever."

CONTENTS

ACKNOWLEDGMENTS

Sincere thanks to:

John Hansen for guiding us through the building process and for providing knowledge and expertise.

Gene and Joanie McConnell for their friendship, prayers and support.

Jerry and Jenny Crossman for continuing to be our friends in the midst of this project.

Pam Houston and Dottie Stephenson for their continual intercession on our behalf.

Alan and Ginny Lukei, whose friendship and love has blessed our lives.

John and Sue, Don and Mary, J.A.C. and Leanne, whose prayers supported us and provided a strength beyond ourselves.

Jean Bryant for her editing skills, and Michelle Treiber for her cover concept.

All those at Here's Life Publishers who encouraged us to write a book together.

Many couples who have shared their personal stories with us, prompting us to complete this book.

FOREWORD

by Josh McDowell

I met Jan Frank in July 1987 at the Christian Booksellers Convention. When she stood up to speak, I was deeply impressed by her testimony. She briefly described her newly released book, *A Door of Hope,* which told the story of her sexual victimization as a child and her subsequent journey toward wholeness. Since I read her book, I have been astonished at the number of young people I encounter who have experienced similar tragedy.

This second book, *When Victims Marry,* is a practical yet compassionate look at the problems couples face when either or both of them come from an abusive background. Jan and her husband Don openly share their own struggles in marriage and their victories as they have worked toward becoming "one flesh."

The book teaches couples how to identify ways in which their individual pasts affect their current relationships. It also shows how to "remove the debris" that prevents proper bonding, and how God can "pour a new foundation" on which to build a strong, secure, sound marriage.

This book is not just for married couples. It will also enlighten and encourage single adults who desire healthy relationships — and engaged couples who want to avoid predictable pitfalls in marriage will find it a valuable guide as well.

The authors draw upon their own personal experience. At the same time, they base their principles on the solidarity of the Word of God and His power to transform and heal troubled relationships.

This is a book of real encouragement for all who desire deeper intimacy and greater unity with their mates.

INTRODUCTION

Brett's voice had a sense of urgency about it. He had heard me the day before on a radio program and my interview had hit home. "I wish I had talked to you months ago," he said. "I never understood, until hearing you yesterday, that my wife's past had anything to do with our marriage problems. Now I'm afraid it's too late." Brett sighed in despair, and continued, "She's living with another man and, although she knows this is not the solution, it is difficult for her to get out of that relationship."

"I understand," I said with compassion. "I receive many phone calls and letters from men who are in similar situations. The important thing for you, Brett, is that you not give up hope. Men in this position must maintain a balance. You need to be supportive and to encourage your wife to seek help, but you also need to be willing to look into your own background. You need to determine what unresolved issues you still carry. You can't allow your wife to walk all over you, but neither can you heavy-handedly try to control her or the circumstances. Does that make sense?"

"Yes," Brett said knowingly. "I made the mistake of trying to force her to get help when she wasn't ready. All that did was make her more angry toward me. More recently," he continued, "I found myself trying to accommodate her every need. Whenever she calls, night or day, I come running—but I just can't live like this anymore."

Brett's story is not unusual. Thousands of couples experience difficulties in their relationships with no clue as to where the roots of the problems are. Struggles over issues like communication, sex, finances, parenting, spiritual leadership, conflict resolution and intimacy continually come to the forefront. These conflicts usually are treated by counselors as present-day concerns that have little to do with one's past, but we have discovered, in our own case and in working with many other couples, that our individual childhood backgrounds have a great deal to do with how we relate with each other. We have seen innumerable cases where the threads of the past have been woven intricately into the tapestry of today's relationships.

As we prayed about writing this book, we wanted to offer hope to many like Brett whose marriages are about to crumble. We believe God wants to restore the foundations in all of our lives and that He designed marriage to be fulfilling for us as well as a symbol of the "oneness" of Christ's relationship with us as believers.

In this book we have attempted to share with you some of what we discovered in our relationship and some of what we've learned from experiences of those we have counseled, along with some fundamental, biblical principles that will help you build a solid, secure, stable marriage foundation. We have included pertinent information for singles and divorced individuals who want to prepare themselves for healthy relationships and avoid dysfunctional entanglements that lead to disillusionment and discouragement.

We have discovered a number of common patterns of struggle that occur when victims marry. We also found that building a marriage is like building a home. God gives some detailed blueprints in His Word, and He says in Psalm 127:1, "Unless the LORD builds the house, they labor in vain who build it."

We will share with you how our relationship has had to go through a rebuilding process. We will take you through the steps of checking your foundation, obtaining a soil report, framing your house, making periodic inspections and "plumbing" checks, and examining your roof for leaks. All this will help you dwell together in unity.

We have seen God faithfully work in our lives to

"build the old waste places" (Isaiah 58:2) and bring us into unity with each other and with Him.

As a result of self-examination and communication, and through yielding ourselves to each other and to God's way in our lives, we have experienced tremendous healing in our own relationship! We have based our belief on His Word, and we are challenged and encouraged continually to allow the Holy Spirit to build in us that ideal "one-flesh" relationship

> Through skillful and godly Wisdom is a house [a life, a home, a family built], and by understanding it is established [on a sound and good foundation]. And by knowledge shall the chambers [of its every area] be filled with all precious and pleasant riches (Proverbs 24:3,4, AMP).

As you begin to read, ask the Holy Spirit to provide you with the wisdom, understanding and knowledge necessary to build your marriage. Remember, no construction project is undertaken without a cost.

Are you ready? We had to start by looking at our own faulty foundations.

1a

Faulty Foundations– Jan

My grandpa, who recently died at a hundred years of age, used to love to tell a story about when I was a child. My grandmother, Rosie Nell, was a preacher of sorts and conducted church services in their home on Sunday. One weekend I had spent Saturday night at their home and got up early Sunday morning to attend Grandma's service. I can still hear her sitting at that old black upright piano singing, "There is pow'r, pow'r, wonder-working pow'r in the blo-o-od of the La-a-amb . . . "

Grandpa would say, "One mornin' Sister Kinnel was supposed to bring the message, but she called up sayin' she was ill. Your grandma looked you in the eye, Jan, and asked if you'd like to deliver the message that mornin'. With a real thoughtful look on your face, you said, 'Yes, but I'll have to prepare.'

"You marched off, so grown up, into the other room, takin' a Bible with you. Pretty soon you came back into the front room and delivered a message to about twenty people who were gathered there.

17

"Later that day, Sister Kinnel called to see what had happened. Your grandma said so proud, 'Why, my grand-daughter brought the message this mornin'.'

"Sister Kinnel was quite amazed and asked, 'Well, what did she preach on?'

"I don't rightly remember what it was, but it was the exact same text that Sister Kinnel had prepared for that day. Your grandma knew right then what you was to do, and she took you up on her lap and told you that day that you'd carry on her preachin' legacy in the family. I know she'd be so proud to be seein' you do just that!"

THE ENEMY

At that tender age, I had no idea what was in store for me, but how thankful I am now that this godly woman faithfully prayed for me. My grandmother died one week before she and my grandfather would have celebrated their 71st wedding anniversary. She died not knowing how the enemy would try to destroy the calling and godly heritage she had prophesied. She died having no idea what had taken place just a few short years after I delivered that message in her living room. She died unaware that a part of her granddaughter had died too, prematurely, at the age of ten.

I was the youngest of three girls, and my parents divorced when I was five. Years later I discovered my mother had married my father when she was just fifteen and my dad was ten years her senior. They had stayed married for fifteen years, although there was a great deal of conflict in their relationship, particularly over finances. My mother always worked, so it was necessary to find house-keepers to care for us girls and to see that the household was intact. I remember only bits and pieces from those early years, although I do recall our housekeeper named Dowie who worked for us nearly ten years. My mother tells me now that Dowie was the one who took care of me from birth, since Mother took off the prescribed six weeks and then returned to work.

I experienced several significant separations before I was eight years old. I "lost" my mother at six weeks, my father at five years, my nanny shortly thereafter, and my oldest sister married and left home when I was seven. Recognizing those losses has helped me understand why bonding and developing intimate relationships have been difficult for me as an adult.

After my parents divorced, we moved to an apartment near my elementary school. Because mother worked to support us, I had little supervision other than what my two sisters provided. I was a lonely child. I did well in school, but I felt a great deal of rejection by my peers. I found myself lying about my family to impress my schoolmates. No one was really aware of how much I hurt inside.

My mother began dating during this time and eventually married my stepfather when I was eight. He had been married previously for nearly twenty years but had no children. He was reared in a Christian home from about age seven. Very different from my natural father, he had a military background and little tolerance for children who did not know how to behave. One of the most significant changes made in our home due to his influence was our weekly church attendance. At one time my stepfather had been a deacon in a fundamental, Bible-believing church and felt it important that we attend church regularly as a family. This was a positive experience for me. It was through our church involvement that I began to hear on a regular basis how Jesus Christ loved me and died for me.

MEETING THE SAVIOR

During an evening service at the age of ten, I raised my hand at the invitation of the evangelist, and I asked Jesus Christ to come into my heart and be my Savior. That night, January 17, 1965, was life-changing. I knew, even at that young age, that my name was written in the Book of

Life and that I would no longer be the same. The evangelist asked all those who had made a commitment to go to the prayer room afterward. My parents had not attended church that evening, so it was just my sister and me. I went to the prayer room, was counseled and prayed with, and then went out to the car where my stepfather was waiting.

As I got into the car he growled, "Where have you been? I've been waiting here for twenty minutes!"

"Dad," I said with eternity's joy bursting from my ten-year-old heart, "I asked Jesus into my heart tonight!"

With a cold, cruel voice he retorted, "Why didn't you wait until your mother and I were there?"

I don't remember making any reply. It wasn't until years later that I felt the impact of his response. He had taken the most important decision I would ever make in my whole life and turned it into something bad. I did not feel the presence of my Jesus at that moment, but I know now that He was there. I also know He grieved over the harshness of my stepfather's response, yet He rejoiced and delighted in me. I was His little lamb — now and forever in the palm of His hand.

A TRAUMATIC EXPERIENCE

Just three weeks later, my mother and sister were at a mother-daughter tea at church. My stepfather called me out of my room on the pretense of watching television with him, and he proceeded to molest me. This also was a life-changing event although I did not realize its significance for nearly twenty years. I have often been asked if this was the only time this occurred. It was not. There were other times prior to this that I remembered only as a result of obtaining counseling years later.

My mother approached me about a month after this happened and asked if anything took place with my stepfather. I did not know then that he was also molesting my older sister. She had gone to my mother, which prompted my mother's questioning me. I told my mother what had taken place and I never heard another word about it. In the mind of a ten-year-old girl, that was just the way life was. I did not learn until adulthood that the abuse continued extensively with my sister, although my stepdad became more subtle and less overt in his actions toward me.

COVERING UP

I did what many victims do — I put those events out of my mind and got on with life. Our family continued to sit in the pew Sunday after Sunday, portraying an image of the model Christian family. No one saw us as an isolated family who rarely let others into our home. No one saw the rigidity, the abuse of power, or the sexual perversion that existed behind the walls. No one saw the sadness in the eyes of a little ten-year-old girl who didn't understand how all this affected her. That little girl did her best to cover it up and pretend it didn't hurt. She tried to make up for it by overachieving in school, and she played that role successfully for several years.

During high school, I covered my deep insecurities by being involved in student activities. I was active in our Christian Life Club on campus, became president of our National Honor Society, and was a cheerleader in my junior and senior years. Due to my insecurities, it was hard for me to develop relationships. I had several friends, but only a few who were close. I had no difficulty establishing relationships with young men, though. Unfortunately, two distinct patterns followed me into adulthood: I was attracted to young men who were either (1) emotionally abusive or (2) weak, passive individuals whom I could control and manipulate. I did not recognize any patterns then, but came to realize later how much they stemmed from my victimization.

I graduated from high school and began attending a state college in our town. This particular period of my life was the rockiest. I became rebellious toward my parents, put my Christian life on hold, and decided to do things my way. I was angry, but I really did not know what about. I was tired of doing things my parents' way and was fed up with trying to please others. The overt sexual abuse had stopped but the subtleties, the innuendos, the sexual perverseness lingered in our home. I became involved in several unhealthy relationships during this time. The past that had long been forgotten was resurrecting itself in my everyday life. I had no idea what was occurring. I was miserable, but knew no way out.

I graduated from college with a bachelor's degree in psychology and began working at a juvenile hall as a counselor for abused, neglected and delinquent youth. I had known since I was fourteen that I wanted to work with troubled young people.

THE TRUTH

At the age of twenty-one, working in that environment, I realized for the first time in my life that what my stepfather had done to me was a criminal offense. I saw my anger reflected in the faces of many young girls who had come to our facility as wards of the court. I grieve now over the shallowness of some of the staff's response to these girls, the lack of our understanding of the devastation in the heart of an abused child. We often were so caught up in their acting-out behavior, their open seductiveness, their anger, and their manipulative styles that we didn't take the time to say, "It wasn't your fault. You are not to blame. The adult who abused you holds the full responsibility."

A FAITHFUL COUPLE

Sometimes I was able to share with girls who would come in screaming, "But you don't know what it's like!" In a way, God was already redeeming some of my past. I only wish I would have known then what I know now.

God used my juvenile hall experience in many ways. In the midst of my rebellion, His Holy Spirit was determined to woo me back to my Savior. I worked with a dedicated Christian man whom I respected. I believe now that Bill must have known what a shambles my life was, yet he loved me with an unconditional love. I know now that many a night, after he got home from work, he and his wife Pat knelt down to pray for a confused young woman who had strayed from her first love.

How thankful I am for the faithfulness of this one couple. The struggle within me was an intense one, and the enemy had convinced me it was too late to go back; I'd gone too far. I'd been too rebellious, too bad, to ever go back. I can still feel the agony of those years away from my Savior — the most lonely time in my entire life.

A RECOMMITMENT

God even used some non-Christian co-workers in the process. Three staff members I worked with let me have it one evening at work. They told me I was a miserable, selfish, angry person they had no desire to have friendship with.

I could hardly believe my ears. I had never been told such things in my life. That night, September 9, 1974, I went home, got down on my knees, and said, "Lord, it's true. This is what my life is without You. If You can do anything with the mess I have made, I'm Yours."

That was a turning point, but it was not instantaneous. Slowly, I began my journey back to a life centered around my Lord and His will for me.

Soon after my recommitment, I started attending a church where the Word of God was taught and believed. I became involved, attending weekly Bible studies and establishing friendships with others my own age. This church was instrumental in laying a strong foundation for me in God's Word. Here I learned about worship and about developing an intimate relationship with my Lord. Although I grew tremendously, I was still unaware of how much I was in bondage to the wounds of the past. As I look back now, I realize that God was preparing me, through establishing me in His Word, to face the hurts of my childhood. It was the growth in my inner spirit and learning about the walk of faith that would eventually allow me to trust God enough to allow myself to explore my past.

HOPE

When Don and I married ten years ago, we had no idea that we were two fractured individuals. (He describes his background in chapter 1b.) We loved each other and were committed to the Lord Jesus Christ. We desired to center our relationship and our home and family on the principles of God's Word.

About two years into our marriage, I began to sense that God was going to restore the fractured foundation of my life. He started by excavating my background. Trapped inside each of us is a wounded boy or girl, held in bondage to the pains of our past. When victims marry, they bring the wounded parts of themselves into the marital relationship. Jesus came to heal the broken-hearted and to set the captives free (see Luke 4:18). He wants to "raise up the foundations of many generations" (Isaiah 58:12).

If you are willing, He is able.

Hope for the wounded boy
trapped inside each man

1b

Faulty Foundations– Don

It was a typical Southern California autumn Saturday morning. Heather, five, and Kellie, three, were ready to enjoy an exciting outing with me. We were especially excited to be going to the Rose Bowl to see the UCLA Bruins play the Arizona Wildcats. We packed a picnic lunch and waited for our companions for the day, Jon and his two sons. We had a great time cheering for the Bruins.

At half time, Jon told me his wife Sharon wanted to call my wife Jan for a counseling referral. He explained that Sharon had been struggling with a great deal of anger and that she had been supercritical of him lately. Jon seemed relieved about Sharon seeking help. He said, "You know, SHE really has a problem."

I reflected on his comment for a moment and looked him right in the eye and said, "You know what, Jon? You've got a problem, too."

Jon didn't like my response and retorted, "What do you mean, I've got a problem?"

I simply said, "Jon, I know just what you're going through . . . I've been there."

DON'S PROBLEMS

Jon's problem, like mine, wasn't just the fact that his wife had been a victim of an abusive childhood. Jon was like me in another way, too. We were both children of alcoholics.

For the past twenty years, I have had the privilege of coaching basketball. As an athletic coach, it is often my job to tell an athlete something that he does not really want to hear. In order for him to improve his game, though, and to help make us a better team, he must hear the truth and then act on it. If he has a flawed jumpshot or his defensive fundamentals are poor, he needs to know about it. If an athlete really desires to improve, he will institute the changes necessary to achieve a higher level of performance.

When Jon claimed it was his wife who had the problem, it reminded me of my initial response to Jan. Early in our marriage, Jan had difficulty trusting me and we were having problems sexually. I saw all our problems as stemming from her past victimization. I did not realize how much being an adult child of an alcoholic (ACA) had to do with our marital relationship. When I began to see that there were unresolved issues in my life that had adversely affected our marriage, I knew I could not place all the responsibility on Jan.

Unspoken Rules

My father was an officer in the Navy and was away from home much of the time. I remember the first time I ever saw my dad — I was five years old and he had come back from the Korean War. From the time he came through the door in his dress blues until now, he has had a drinking problem. We never called it a drinking problem. We didn't talk about it at all — until I was twenty-seven.

One of the basic unspoken rules of an alcoholic home is: "Don't talk." In fact, in her book, *It Will Never Happen to Me,* Claudia Black states that the credo of the alcoholic home is: "Don't talk; don't trust; don't feel."[1]

As a boy I would lie in bed at night listening to my parents argue about Dad's drinking. I was scared to death that my dad would hit my mom, and I wondered if it were my fault they were arguing. All my six brothers and sisters heard the arguing, too, but no one ever talked about it the next day. Most alcoholic families fall into similar patterns.

Sarcasm

When my family did communicate, we used tremendous, unmerciful sarcasm with one another. I saw nothing wrong with that and was proud of my family, so I took Jan to family get-togethers when we were dating. It wasn't until she pointed out the sarcasm that I really became aware of it. The word *sarcasm* literally means to "tear or rip away flesh." We were tearing each other apart with our words.

Unfortunately, every once in a while, this pattern of sarcasm still emerges. Recently at a Labor Day get-together with my family, we started playing Trivial Pursuit. When we started we each wanted to get the competitive edge, and the ripping began again. I was as sarcastic and intimidating as anyone there. The sad part was that my two daughters were there also, listening to their father.

Jan and I had two agreements before we got married. The first was to pay off our Mastercards and not use them again. The second was not to use sarcasm. We agreed to point it out to each other any time we heard the other one using it. Jan had to call me on my behavior that Labor Day afternoon. I was guilty as charged, and I knew it. I had let an old negative family pattern re-emerge.

Hidden Feelings

Along with the sarcasm problem, telling anyone what I am feeling deep inside has been difficult. Like most

ACAs I had little ability to put words to my feelings. We were never allowed to talk about feelings in my family so we never learned how. The emotional part of me was not nurtured and did not develop in a healthy way. In response to Jan's questions about how I felt about something, I would often struggle inside, trying to figure out what I was feeling and how I could express it.

Patterns established in childhood are often difficult to change. Chuck Swindoll said in a sermon once, "The church cannot resurrect what the home has put to death."

I began to attend a support group at my church for adult children of alcoholics. It helped to share common experiences with others. This gave me the chance to explore some of the feelings I had buried. For the first time, many of us vented the anger we felt about growing up in such dysfunctional homes. I had a father—but I never really had a father, not like my friends had. My father didn't take time for me. We never golfed, camped, fished or played ball.

Ridicule and Humiliation

Many ACAs have a hard time having fun. We don't like to socialize because we don't know what to say. Opening up to others scares us. We hold our emotions in, and oftentimes, beneath our easy-going appearance, we hide a reservoir of rage. The anger comes from being deprived of the kind of home life others seem to have had and we feel we were cheated. Many of us do not even realize, until we reach adulthood, that we have harbored this resentment.

Another source of the anger we feel is abandonment and broken promises. As an ACA, life was unpredictable and harsh. I was often the target of my father's ridicule.

When I was a young boy between seven and eight, we lived in Sasebo, Japan, where my father was serving in the U. S. Navy. It was a neat experience and mostly filled with good memories. Since my father was an officer, we were accorded many extra benefits, one of which was access to a golf course on the base. My mom and dad took up golf.

Since I loved sports, I was glad when my father asked me to caddie for him one day. That day he played with three other officer friends. He had handed me his wristwatch to take care of while he was playing, but like any normal eight-year-old boy, I got a little restless. On the 16th hole, I went walking along the shore of the Sea of Japan to find a few rocks to skip. I can still see the watch flying off my wrist, hitting a rock and smashing into pieces as I skipped that first rock on the water. My father didn't see it happen, so I was faced with having to tell him about it. I don't know if he had been drinking at the time, but I do remember how he cursed at me and gave me a swift kick in the pants in front of his three friends. I was deeply humiliated.

As an adult reflecting on this incident, I have had a mixture of emotions. I have felt deeply sad when I realized this was one of the few times my dad and I did anything together. I also have felt anger for the way Dad publicly humiliated me.

Others' Anger

Most ACAs have trouble being around angry people. They want to get away so nothing bad will happen. I have been no different.

Anger scares me so much and makes me feel so helpless and out of control that I find it difficult to let Jan vent legitimate anger. This is not healthy for our relationship. When she is angry, I usually respond by doing something productive. I iron some clothes, do the laundry or clean up the garage. I perform compulsively to make amends for the situation. Some of you wives might be saying, "I wish my husband would do that! Maybe we'd get some work done around here!" The fact is, I am trying to avoid a confrontation and simply want to earn my way back into my wife's good graces. I really should just allow her to be mad.

I've recognized this pattern and am working to break

these destructive habits. Confrontation is something I usually want no part of. My motto has been, "If you leave it alone, maybe it will get fixed or go away by itself." Maintaining this motto in our marriage has not been easy. Jan and I come from different molds. She sees a problem and wants to address it immediately. If I see a problem, I hope it will disappear before we have to confront it. We each have had to adjust considerably in this area.

Maintaining Control

Another major issue for an ACA is control. Since we grew up in an environment that was essentially out of control and unpredictable, we panic if we feel we are losing our grip on a situation. As a school teacher, I have always been rated high in classroom control. I do a nice job in front of a group. To look at me, you would probably think I have everything in order. Inside I feel I *must* have things in check, because if I don't, I'm scared to death. Unpredictable events or changes in my schedule can throw me into a panic.

Control is a prominent issue also for a victim of incest. Jan lived in another environment that was out of control. Think of the clashing that takes place when two people from these backgrounds get together as "one flesh." It doesn't take a genius to figure out that these people will suffer when they try to establish a solid relationship.

We all have brought things into our marriage that we don't want to admit are part of the problem. In my case, it was coming from a dysfunctional alcoholic home. I had learned some unhealthy patterns. When Jan started seeing a counselor about her victimization, I thought everything would be great, because she'd get fixed. That was the wrong attitude. It wasn't until I recognized my responsibility in the relationship that progress was made.

Below are some common characteristics of those who grow up in an alcoholic or "dry" alcoholic home. In the dry alcoholic home, the parents are not alcoholics, but one

of their parents or grandparents was. Though active drinking has not been in the family for some time, the family dynamics, the rules and behaviors, continue in a way charactistic of an actively drinking alcoholic family.

If you can relate to these personality attributes but don't remember your parents abusing alcohol, you probably fit into the dry alcoholic category. If you find that you do relate, there are some good books and support groups available for you. Get involved in your own recovery.

ACA Characteristics[2]

1. ACAs do not know what normal is. We were brought up in an abnormal environment and have believed it was normal.
2. ACAs have great difficulty having fun.
3. ACAs are serious people. Don't joke around with an ACA; we usually don't like it.
4. ACAs overreact to changes over which we have no control.
5. ACAs like to have people affirm us and will work hard for praise.
6. ACAs like to criticize other people.
7. ACAs are loyal, even in the face of evidence that the loyalty is undeserved.
8. ACAs have an inability to open up to others.
9. ACAs judge themselves without mercy.
10. ACAs have difficulty with intimate relationships.
11. ACAs are either super-responsible or super-irresponsible.
12. ACAs are impulsive.

Only in the last four years have I realized how deeply I was affected by my alcoholic family. I was previously indifferent to the damages in my foundation that contributed to the instability of our marital relationship. As I have been open to the Holy Spirit, whose job is to lead us "into all truth," and have educated myself, God has been faithful to repair the structural damage from my past.

OTHER FAULTY FOUNDATIONS – Jan

Some of you can relate totally to what Don and I have shared, but you do not see yourself in the categories of the abused or coming from an alcoholic home. If you have trouble building intimacy, if you experience explosive anger at times, if you tend to have a negative view of life, or if you panic when a situation gets out of your control, you may need to take a closer look at your own foundations, your own family history.

We have found that victims tend to marry victims, but that those who were victimized or who suffered some childhood trauma or loss often have difficulty recognizing the impact those events still have on their adult life. The only way to recognize that impact is by the symptoms. It is much like cancer. You may have it but show very few signs in the beginning stages. This does not mean it is not there. A doctor who sees certain consistent symptoms can finally accurately diagnose the condition. So it is with emotional symptoms. If you identify with some of what you have read, or if your spouse has observed some of these symptoms in your life, you need to examine your foundations.

If a woman has been a victim of abuse (physical, emotional or sexual) in her childhood, she tends to marry someone from one of four types of backgrounds: first, one of abuse (physical, emotional or sexual); second, an alcoholic or dry alcoholic home; third, what I call a "rigid," often strictly religious, home; or fourth, a home background where the person was emotionally deprived. Let's look at these categories a little more closely.

The Home Where Abuse Occurred

In working with men, we have found that – in our

culture—it is not acceptable for them to be identified as, or admit to being, victims of abuse. For instance, if I ask a group of men if they were ever sexually victimized in childhood, 90 percent will say no. However, if I ask those same men if they ever had a "sexual encounter" as a boy or young man, 80 percent say yes. Many times men rationalize away such abuse as "normal childhood encounters." True, not all such encounters classify as abuse, but too many do.

The same is true for men who were physically or emotionally abused in their home. They look back on what occurred and often do not recognize the verbal harangues, harsh physical treatment or emotional cruelty they were subjected to as abuse. It was "just the way we were raised." Most of us have no reference point with which to compare, so we assume we were raised normally, when we actually grew up in an abnormal, unhealthy home.

The Alcoholic or Dry Alcoholic Home

It seems the alcoholic home would be easy to detect, but that is not always the case. The same is true of the dry alcoholic home. Characteristic of this home is the dysfunctional credo Don talked about earlier—you learn as a child: "Don't talk; don't trust; don't feel." The strong system of family loyalty held to by the alcoholic or dry alcoholic home is maintained by denial. Most family members appear to be close and loving, but in truth they are bound to the family secrets, unable to escape the "good family" image.

The Rigid Home

The rigid, sometimes religious, home is the hardest of all to spot. The children are usually well-behaved because adherence to rules is so much more important than communicating love. The child learns to perform as a means of obtaining approval. This produces an adult who compulsively performs and equates productivity with personal value.

The Emotionally Deprived Home

This home can look so good on the outside, but inside the children grow up feeling unloved and emotionally deprived. Here, the child *learns* he is loved by what has been provided for him, but he does not *feel* loved. His emotional needs have been overlooked, and physical provisions have been made instead. Men or women who grew up in this type of environment have difficulty building intimacy with their spouses because intimacy and nurturing were missing for them when they were children. If you grew up in this type of home, you may find it hard to be a loving parent to your own children or to feel emotionally close to your mate.

Not all men who marry women who were sexually abused fit into the four categories listed above, but many do. If you are one who does not, I still encourage you to take an honest look at the home in which you were raised.

Actually, all of us grew up in dysfunctional families to some degree — we are all imperfect products of imperfect parents. The Scriptures give several examples of godly men and women who made mistakes parenting their children, for example: Eli, Samuel, David and Rebecca. As a result of these people's parenting, their children suffered character flaws, "symptoms" that followed them into adulthood, affecting their lives — and how they in turn would parent.

IDENTIFYING SYMPTOMS

Take a few minutes and think about the following questions. If some of these experiences describe your growing-up years, you may be sure they are reflected in the way you deal with life — and in your relationships with others and with God.

- Did you lose a parent by either divorce or death?
- Were either of your parents absent from home a great deal?
- Was one of your parents critical or perfectionistic?

- Did either parent look to you to be his or her confidant?
- Were you strongly tied to one parent?
- Is it difficult for you to hear your mate or siblings express any negative comments about your family of origin?
- Were your feelings acknowledged and validated?

We are not advocating that you look into your background for the purpose of blaming. We simply encourage you to see the truth of where you came from so you can see better where you want to go.

We all have three options: (1) We can spend a lifetime blaming our current condition on our past; (2) we can ignore our past and its results in our present; or (3) we can go through the PROCESS of healing our past in order to set our present free.

Deuteronomy 32:7 says: "Remember the days of old, consider the years of many generations. Ask your father, and he will show you; your elders, and they will tell you." Although God admonishes the Israelites to review His faithfulness in this verse, there is another principle here that we should not overlook.

We are to survey our foundations wisely that we might repair the fractures and provide stability and security for our families, and for their families in the future.

*Discovering hidden background differences
that shape your relationship*

2

*Preparing
the Soil*

The phone rang in my apartment one wintry evening about two years after Don and I had met. It was Don. There was a deep concern in his voice. Over the next few minutes he related several facts about his father that had recently begun to trouble him. There I sat, only twenty-four years old, being confronted with Don's family's dark secrets. We were not dating at the time, but he called to get my advice. He knew I worked with people in probation who often had drug-related problems, and I remember him asking if I thought his father had an alcohol problem.

He described several incidents from the past ten years, and I responded, "From what you have told me, it's clear your father is an alcoholic." There was silence on the other end for a long moment. Then we talked some more and I suggested different organizations that might be helpful. I made several calls myself during the next few days, and even recommended that the family get together to conduct an alcoholic intervention. I could tell Don was in a great deal of distress, but I had no idea how much his father's problem and his family's denial would later affect the two of us.

"MARRYING HIS FAMILY"

It is interesting that we enter into serious relationships with so little knowledge of how our backgrounds will influence our personal affairs. We are often told in jest before we marry, "You are not just marrying the person; you are marrying his (or her) family as well." Somehow we hear those words and rationalize away the true force of their meaning. I remember how thankful I was, when Don proposed, that he was a Christian dedicated to God's will in his life, and that I probably never would have to deal with what his mother has for more than thirty years. How naive I was to think that Don had escaped the effect of his father's alcoholism and that his family dysfunction was not a problem to him just because he was a Christian.

In my own life, I was aware of some unhealthy patterns in my family, but I just decided that in raising my own children I would do things differently. Unfortunately, there were several patterns I was not aware of. Then I discovered, once I married, that even the patterns I did know about were not as simple to change as I had imagined.

Isn't it enough that two people are committed to their God, and love one another, and marry with good intentions? As I reflected on this question, I asked myself, *This seems like it should be enough, but is it really?*

God drew me to the Scriptures, especially in reference to building a house. Psalm 127:1 says: "Unless the LORD build the house, they labor in vain that build it." I began thinking about this verse in the full context of building a house when I talked to a few building contractor friends.

THE SOIL REPORT

One of these friends, John, told me that usually the first step taken when one decides to build a house is to obtain a soil report. "A soil report?" I asked. "What in the world is that for?"

He explained that before a foundation can be laid, the soil upon which the house is to sit must be tested. A specialist goes to the land site and conducts several digs to determine what type of soil is there.

My friend said, "It is important to determine that the ground is properly compacted. For example, sometimes the particular spot is found to have been a dump site years before. If you try to build on it, the foundation will not be firm enough and the structure will not hold."

I was intrigued by this.

He continued, "The soils engineer has to make sure the ground is compacted in order to avoid slippage. He will do several different tests in several locations and at different depths, and if the soil is not right, he will see that the builder does what is necessary to bring it up to standard before the foundation is laid."

As I thought about this concept, I was amazed. I likened the whole building process to a marriage. How often we try to build our marriage on a faulty foundation. A soil report would require us to look into our individual backgrounds and determine what kind of ground we are trying to build on—and we fail to obtain that vital report. I realized what God was saying in Psalm 127:1.

He is not just interested in the structure of the house itself, but He wants us to include Him in every aspect of the building project and to center our marriage house in His hands. In practical terms, that means we submit the soil from our individual backgrounds to Him for inspection. Ideally, this would occur before we enter the marital bond. Unfortunately, in most cases it does not. Instead, we rush ahead and build our marriage on soil that has not been prepared properly. Then years down the road the "house" begins to deteriorate.

We have seen so many instances of this. We have counseled numerous fine Christian couples who truly love the Lord but who in ignorance started building their house without first submitting their soil to the Master Builder for His report. We found ourselves in that state, too.

HOW THE PATTERNS AFFECT US

I had told Don before we married about the incest within my childhood home. Neither of us had any idea what kind of impact the events of twenty years earlier would have on us. I did not realize that the dysfunctional patterns of his and my individual families were so much alike, and that these patterns would play a significant role in how our house would be built.

About two years into our marriage the structural damage began to appear. As with a house, things did not fall apart all at once. Initially it was subtle. We had bought a lovely condominium and were both working. Signs of damage showed up early in our marriage, but I viewed them as adjustments to married life.

One incident particularly comes to mind. Shortly after we married, Don enrolled in a master's program in education that required two nights a week away from home. He also coached a basketball team, which made a lot of demands on his time. I would often sit at home those nights in a carefully controlled depression. Then one evening it erupted. I burst into tears as he headed for the door.

"You don't understand," I cried. "It's been easy for you. I moved forty miles away from my home, my church, my friends. Now I have a new husband, a new home and a new job—but nothing has changed for you," I accused. "You still have all your old buddies calling you to go watch a ball game. Do you realize I don't have anyone I can call without it being long distance?"

Don didn't know how to respond. He tried the best he could to be sensitive to my needs. Neither of us had recognized that effects of the earlier trauma were creeping to the surface. My complaints sounded somewhat normal for a new bride, so I had tried to rationalize my unhappiness away, telling myself I just needed more time to adjust.

Then the structure of our marriage showed a new crack as another issue came to light. I was extremely jealous. If Don and I went shopping, and I would see him looking around, I just knew he was looking at another woman.

One day he came home from work and told me about one of the secretaries. He described her attractiveness and related an innocent encounter she'd had with another staff worker. My internal wheels started spinning. As I sat there listening, a voice inside started saying, *Don really likes this woman. He probably wishes he would have married her rather than you.* I could not shut that voice off.

I found myself asking him questions about her almost daily. I looked for signs that might indicate how involved he had gotten with her. I looked in his pockets for notes or some other type of evidence. Before long, everywhere we went I found myself watching him watch other women. Inside I was angry. I convinced myself he would have an affair.

One day Don could not take the innuendos or subtle accusations anymore. He looked me straight in the eye and said, "Jan, you will get from me what you expect. If you expect me to go out and have an affair, I will probably do it. But if you trust me to be faithful, and stop inferring things that are not true, I will live up to that commitment."

I broke down in tears. "Honey, you don't know how hard that is for me. Every man I ever trusted has done me dirt. Why should I expect anything different from you?"

Lovingly, but firmly, Don said, "If you will just trust me, with no reservations, I will prove to you that I am trustworthy."

That was a turning point in that particular area. I remember sitting with Don on the bed telling him I would, from that day on, with God's help, begin to trust him. One crack in our structure was temporarily sealed.

THREE AREAS OF STRUGGLE

With the birth of our first daughter, Heather, the structure could no longer maintain its equilibrium. Within a very short time I was emotionally leveled as God worked to get my attention. I struggled with three distinct problem areas. I now know them as symptoms.

Depression

First, I was mildly depressed much of the time— nothing excited me. I was down in the mouth about life in general. I thought it was due to our tight financial situation and the stresses of being a new mother, so I expected it simply to disappear after I adjusted.

Anger

The second symptom, the most distressing one, was anger. I still recall bringing Heather home from the hospital and that very first night being awakened to her cry. I picked her up, changed her diaper and fed her. Then I put her in her crib and dragged my tired body back to bed. Within fifteen minutes she was crying again. I got up, took her downstairs to try to rock her to sleep. She continued to cry. I walked her, sang to her, patted her, checked her diaper—all to no avail. She kept crying and crying and crying.

I began to pray. "Lord, please let her stop crying. I am so tired. I need some sleep." She cried more. Suddenly, anger leaped out of nowhere. "What do you want from me? I don't know what is wrong with you. Will you please stop crying?!"

The voice repeated in my head. I felt like shaking her so she would be quiet. Fear gripped my heart. *What is wrong with me?* I thought.

Finally her colicky stomach settled down. Her crying ceased — but my fear remained. How could I feel so out of control? Where was that anger coming from? More frightening than anything else was the question: What would I do with this anger? I went to bed deeply troubled and ashamed.

A Critical Spirit

The final symptom, the one I would have to face, was my critical spirit toward my husband. Whatever Don would do, I found something wrong with it. He would help me around the house and I would criticize his every move. I would scrutinize his every action and point out everything that did not meet my standards.

One Saturday we decided to go to the beach. Heather was just a toddler at the time, and Don arose early that morning, lovingly got Heather up and dressed, and was feeding her breakfast. I came downstairs and started in. "Why did you put that on her? She can't wear THAT to the beach! . . . How come you gave her so much cereal? She can never eat that much . . . Why don't you help me pack this lunch? Do I always have to do everything?" Later, "Why are we going to THIS beach? . . . Don't park here, I don't want to walk a mile! . . . Do you have to take her in the water NOW? We haven't even had lunch yet . . . I'm tired. Can't we just go home?" By the end of that day, Don felt like he had been through World War III and lost!

I saw I was making him miserable, and in fact, I was miserable myself. I could not get away from the depression or anger, or from being critical. Everywhere I turned I faced one of these symptoms in some form or another. I didn't know where the barrage was coming from, but I knew I wanted to change. I got on my knees and began to plead with God to change me. I confessed that these were areas I did not like about myself and these things were not pleasing to God. I prayed over each area, and begged God to change me. Nothing happened. Weeks went by, but the depression, anger and critical spirit remained. I cried to the Lord, "What's wrong, Lord? I've asked, I've pleaded with You to change me, and nothing has happened. I don't understand."

SUPERFICIAL HEALING

Shortly after this, during my devotions one morning, I found a verse that would prove to be life-changing:

Behold, You desire truth in the inward parts, and in the hidden part You will make me to know wisdom (Psalm 51:6).

That verse gripped my heart and I felt compelled to begin praying the verse daily. As I did, it seemed God's Spirit tenderly spoke to my heart, *The wounds of the past have not been healed.*

I knew exactly what the Lord was referring to, but I rebutted with, "Lord, what else do you want from me? I've done everything I know scripturally to do. I've forgiven my stepdad for what he did to me and I've even asked You to forgive him. What more do you want?"

The Lord immediately brought to my mind an event that had taken place when I was eighteen. I had to have three impacted wisdom teeth removed. As I sat in the oral surgeon's office for a consultation, he discussed the process of the surgery that was set for the following week. I would be under a general anesthetic and he would surgically remove the impacted teeth.

"After the surgery," he continued, "you will swell up like a chipmunk and will be in some pain. I will prescribe some medication to help you through that period. The swelling will go down after about two weeks and by the third week, you will be back to normal."

All the doctor predicted came true, up to the third week following the surgery. The swelling had indeed gone down and the pain was gone at the end of the two weeks, but at the end of the third week, I had pain in my jaw. I wondered what was wrong. I had a choice. I could ignore the pain and convince myself that I was really "back to normal" as I had been assured I would be, or I could investigate the source of the pain. I chose the latter and made an appointment with the surgeon. While sitting in the dental chair, I caught a glimpse of myself in the mirror.

I look fine on the outside, I said to myself, *but I don't feel fine on the inside.* The doctor examined the wound and instantly knew what the problem was.

"Jan," he said, "you have developed what is known as a dry socket."

"What is that?" I questioned.

"The blood clot has dislodged itself from the wound and has left an open area into which food particles and bacteria have entered. In an attempt to heal quickly, your body has covered over that wound with a superficial layer of skin, trapping the infectious material inside. This is what is causing your pain."

"So now what do we do?" I asked squeamishly.

"Unfortunately," he replied, "the solution to the problem is uncomfortable. We must lance the wound and release all that infectious material."

"Isn't there some other way?" I asked.

There wasn't. After the lancing, he handed me a hypodermic needle and said, "Now, for the next two weeks, you are to inject the wound with saline solution three times a day. We need to make sure all the dried blood and bacteria is out of that wound so that it can properly heal." Out of the office I went, needle in hand.

As the Lord brought that experience to my mind, He seemed to be saying, *The wounds of the past have not been healed. You have attempted, Jan, to cover those wounds with a superficial layer of spirituality and forgiveness. It is time we lance the wound. You have attempted to heal yourself from the outside in, but through My Spirit, I am going to heal you totally—this time from the inside out.*

BACK TO THE SOIL

I had no idea of all that was to come. The Lord did not lay it all out before me, but I knew He expected me to trust Him. Something inside me knew He was answering the desperate prayer of this young wife and mother. That was the beginning. We had to go back to the foundations.

Years later, I found a Scripture in Psalm 11:3 that states: "If the foundations be destroyed, what can the righteous do?" I realize now that God is so faithful in our lives that He wants to take us back to the foundations. He knows that to build on anything other than Him will cause a faltering later on. He had to call me to the place of "obtaining a soil report" prior to laying a new foundation in Him. He was prompting me to look, in truth, at the soil upon which I was trying to build a marriage, a family, a home.

Don and I soon discovered many areas which had been dramatically impacted by our family backgrounds. The more we shared with each other, the better we understood the individual differences in how we dealt with everyday issues of marriage and life.

We have found in doing seminars that one of the major breakdowns in marriages is communication. We encourage couples to go on an "expedition" and investigate the content of their "family soil." We provide a series of topics and questions that initiate discussion and discovery.

Recently at a seminar, one woman approached me at the break, after having completed the "expedition" assignment with her husband the night before, and said, "I couldn't believe it! We have been married for over twenty years and I never knew some of the things my husband told me about the way he was raised. It all makes so much sense to me now. No wonder we have struggled so in finances and parenting our kids. We both grew up with such different views of how to handle these areas. To tell you the truth, it was the best conversation we have had in years."

We have provided those questions for you in the chapter on Periodic Inspections, along with our discoveries as we dug into our own family's soil history. No matter what you find, though, know that it is not too late! God is the Master Builder and He delights in "build[ing] the old waste places" in our lives and "rais[ing] up the foundations of many generations" (Isaiah 58:2 and 12).

EXCAVATING THE SOIL

When examining the soil, sometimes the engineers look for contaminants such as hazardous wastes, or hydrocarbons such as petroleum. They realize it would be extremely dangerous to construct a building on such polluted ground. They tell the builder how far to excavate and how much soil must be removed before the foundation footings can be placed. Sometimes the soil can be treated and recompacted to bring it up to proper standards and make it more stable. Other times the soil is so bad it must be removed and new soil brought in. Occasionally, the builder must go all the way to bedrock to find solidarity.

THE LEAVING PRINCIPLE

When victims marry, they often bring contaminants in the "soil" of their lives into the marriage. God has designed certain principles to ensure that a proper foundation will be laid. Genesis 2:24 says: "Therefore a man shall leave his father and mother and be joined to his wife, and they shall become one flesh." Let's look here at the "leaving" principle as it relates to marriage. (We'll examine "cleaving" in the next chapter.)

In *Strike the Original Match* Chuck Swindoll lists four "musts" for marital harmony. These were gleaned from the verse above and from the next verse, Genesis 2:25: "And they were both naked . . . and were not ashamed." The four musts are **severance** (leaving father and mother), **per-**

manence (cleaving to spouse), **unity** (becoming one flesh), and **intimacy** (being naked and not ashamed).

What is involved in severance? Swindoll writes:

> To "leave . . . father and mother" means to break the parent-child bond, to sever the tight, emotionally dependent strings that once provided security, protection, financial assistance and physical needs. All or any of those ties, if brought over into a marriage, will hinder the bond of marriage.[1]

Let's look at the principle of severance in three aspects—body, soul and spirit—to get a clearer picture of the separation that needs to take place.

Physical Severance

First, there is the body, or physical separation, that must occur when a couple unites in marriage. God knew that there must be a physical separation of both partners from their parents for them to truly "cleave" to each other.

Creating physical distance between your parents and in-laws helps to establish the separateness needed for the marital bond to strengthen. Have you ever asked someone who started their marriage in their parents' or in-laws' homes what it was like? Many of them will tell you it was absolutely necessary at the time, but if they had it to do over, they'd find another way.

I know of an older couple, Charles and Mary, who are trying to help their daughter and her husband get on their feet financially. They recently offered to let them move in along with their three children. Mary was determined to make this arrangement work. She sat down with her daughter and defined the guidelines of the household. In order to maintain separate living space, Mary had a contractor come and construct a dividing wall giving separate entrance to her home for herself and her husband.

Although Mary went to extensive measures to try to create a separation, the "house within the house" began to falter. One day her daughter had an argument with her husband, which Mary overheard. Mary was determined to keep out of it, but after her son-in-law stormed out the door, Mary's daughter came running. Mary found herself in the middle. A little later, she volunteered to keep the children while her daughter went shopping with a friend. Before she knew it, her daughter was calling on her more and more to "watch the kids for just a while" so she could get out of the house. Mary soon began to resent the living arrangements. She also observed that her daughter and son-in-law's relationship was deteriorating steadily. Mary felt trapped. Her intentions were good, but somehow the relationship she so desired to support had been undermined.

This does not mean that every married couple who do not establish distance between themselves and their parents are destined to fail, but if the physical nearness reflects emotional dependency, the couple could be headed for trouble. The excavation process must go beyond the physical, to the emotional realm.

Emotional Severance

What if the couple establishes distance from their parents but emotional ties have not been severed? Susan was an only child and had always been close to her parents, but after marrying she moved a good distance away. She appeared to have grown up in an ideal home. I met Susan at a conference and noted the pain in her eyes. After chatting for a while, I asked about her family and her growing-up years.

"Oh, it was like Disneyland. My parents didn't have a lot of money, but I was called the 'princess' even by the extended family. All my cousins loved coming to our house."

As we talked, I realized Susan's parents still played an important role in her life. Although Susan had been married more than fifteen years, her parents visited weekly. Susan had a good marriage and three lovely children. She seemed to have few problems except for her health. She told me she'd had severe stomach aches from the time she was about eight years old.

"Was there anything negative about your childhood?" I asked.

"No, nothing. The only thing I remember was that I didn't want to go to school when I was around eight, so my parents took me to a school psychologist. I begged them not to send me to school, but they were advised there was nothing wrong with me and they should make me go."

The pieces began to fit together. Although I did not share my impressions with Susan, I was sure something had happened to her as a child. She had an unusual attachment to her parents, lapses of memory in childhood, plus what appeared to have been a school phobic reaction at eight. She also suffered colitis, which is common among victims of repressed trauma.

The more Susan shared, the more obvious it became. Her stomach aches had gotten severe about five years before. Now she was hemorrhaging, but there was no medical explanation for it. Her condition was so serious that her doctor had said she must figure out what was causing the stress in her life or she would be in acute danger. A pastor friend observed that Susan's stomach problems seemed to increase on the weekends. He also noted Susan's parents were at her home every weekend. He saw the connection, set Susan and her husband down and counseled them to begin to break some of those ties.

"It almost killed my parents," Susan recalled. "Especially my father. He was totally involved in our lives. We separated from my parents for about nine months. During that time we still talked by phone, but my dad wasn't allowed to just drop in any time he wanted. Now that I think about it, my stomach problems virtually disappeared during that time. I felt incredibly free, but incredibly guilty for what I was putting them through."

"How is your relationship with them now?" I asked.

"Well, they're not here nearly as much, but my stomach still acts up whenever a family get-together is planned. I have noticed a big difference in my relationship with my husband. I can't explain it, but my dad always seemed to come between us. He'd pick apart some business decision my husband made or the way he disciplined the kids. I constantly felt like a mediator. I've been able to focus more on my husband—and that's been great."

I did not know all Susan had experienced in her past; however, it was evident her involvement with her parents, particularly her father, affected her physical health. I encouraged Susan to pray during the summer and ask the Lord for direction.

When fall came Susan entered counseling. After six months of specialized help she began to remember her childhood. Her fear of school now made sense. She remembered that when she was about eight, the school principal had called her into his office and then molested her. More memories came that were much more difficult to cope with. She had been molested around the age of four—this time by her father.

"I couldn't believe it, but I knew it was true," she later told me. "I'll never forget that first day you and I talked. I sensed your concern about my past. I felt panicky and didn't know why. I could not stop crying after I left. The strange thing was, while I felt the panic, I also had an indescribable peace, as though God were bringing me into a new awareness. I wonder if I would have followed through if I had known what I would discover. It has been absolutely life-changing."

Susan eventually confronted her father and told her mother what occurred. Her father denied it. Her mother believed her. Susan has noticed a dramatic change in her physical and emotional health. She set firm boundaries, limiting her contact with her father. She now understands how deeply she was affected by the things she did not even remember.

Sometimes, as in Susan's case, God directs us to excavate what appears to be perfectly good "soil." He sees beyond the top layer to the lower levels where the contaminants lay.

If one or both parties have experienced some type of abuse or dysfunction in the family of origin, it is often difficult for the proper emotional (soul) "leaving" to take place. When Don and I were courting, his emotional attachment to his family became an issue. We had known each other for nearly three years, and our relationship had been rocky. The last year before we got married was particularly rough for me. The Lord had made it clear to me, after some heartbreaking situations, that I had been trying to manipulate and control my relationship with Don. After a lengthy separation, Don came back into my life, and I knew we were to be married. The trouble was, God had not told Don yet. The Lord impressed me to wait on Him and not connive with Don.

Months went by and each weekend I would hope Don would ask me to marry him. I was literally wasting away, weighing in at eighty-eight pounds. I finally had a talk with Don and said I could not go on much longer not knowing our future. He made an appointment for us with his pastor.

Pastor Mike looked Don in the eye and said, "You're not getting any younger. You need to make a decision." He quoted Proverbs 13:12a (KJV): "Hope deferred maketh the heart sick," and he said it was obvious I was suffering from having my hopes deferred.

The pastor said something else that we did not recognize as important at the time, but in retrospect I see the wisdom God gave him. This pastor said, "Don, you've been tied emotionally to your parents. You're thirty years old; if you don't break that tie soon, it will be difficult for you ever to break it."

Pastor Mike knew Don came from an alcoholic home and that, as the oldest boy, he carried a lot of the emotional pain of the family. In many ways, he had been expected to fulfill the man's role since his dad had become increasingly more irresponsible, and he had not broken away from all that.

Many people believe that, because they have separated from their family physically, they have achieved proper severance. However, for those who have been victimized in any way, the severance process has often been incomplete.

Emotional ties are invisible. No one can see the attachment of a man who is still "tied to his mother's apron strings," but we certainly can identify the effects. Sexual abuse and trauma are not the only things that bring about emotional ties. Sometimes these ties are a result of unfinished business or unresolved conflicts.

Unhealthy emotional ties that are not severed are like tree roots that work their way under a foundation and eventually cause it to fracture. When proper severance takes place in the emotional realm, it liberates each partner to bond more intimately, and the foundation is more secure.

Spiritual Severance

Severance must also occur in the area of the spirit. We cannot grow into unity with our mate until we establish our own unique relationship with God, separate from that of our parents. This is particularly difficult for the child who grows up in a Christian home or in a home loyal to a certain faith or denomination. Often that person has never learned how to have a relationship with God on a personal level. Doctrines and ideas about God are passed down that are arbitrarily accepted.

The trouble with that is, you cannot live in a vital relationship with God based on someone else's experience. It's like trying to build your house on another person's foundation. God desires that we cultivate our own individual relationship with Him. As we do, we also solidify our commitment to each other.

———

We have looked at the criterion of severance and have seen how it must occur on all three levels: body, soul and spirit. We have seen that this principle is a prerequisite to cleaving with our mate. God may require excavation into areas that contain hidden contaminants affecting your relationship with your mate and with Him. God has a design and He knows best how it should be implemented. He subcontracts some of the work to us, but provides us with detailed architectural drawings and blueprints.

Now, before we go on in the building process, we must think about the design. If you were building your own home, what would you consider essential? A whirlpool bathtub? A fireplace in the master bedroom? A cozy breakfast nook? We must look to the Designer for His Master plan.

How long has it been since you studied His plans? We'll consult the architect and look at the blueprints in the next chapter.

3

*Who Needs
an Architect?
Or Blueprints?*

We went out early this evening, while it was still light, for a family drive. With our little girls in the back seat, we purposely drove through some classy neighborhoods in our area, developments far beyond our means, to see how the other half lives. We marveled at the beauty of the landscapes and the magnificence of spacious living.

"I'd like to live in that one," Heather commented.

"Oh, look, Mom, that one's for sale. Maybe we can buy it!" Kellie said enthusiastically. Don and I shared a fast glance, smiling at their naiveté.

While admiring the landscapes, style and decor, I thought, *Someone has put a great deal of effort into making all of this come together.*

As we drove up one street Don said, "Wow, look at these custom homes!"

Simultaneously both girls asked, "Dad, what is a custom home?" Don explained that a custom home simply is

different from any other home around. You hire a person
called an architect to design and draw pictures of what the
finished house will look like.

"Can the architect make the house any way he
wants?" asked Heather.

"Not exactly," Don replied. "People tell him their
ideas, and they take him to the piece of land they want to
build on. Once he sees the land and has an idea what they
want, he starts to make drawings and floor plans."

"Do we have a custom home, Daddy?"

"No, girls. We have a tract home. Custom homes are
very expensive."

"Maybe someday we can have a custom one, Dad."
said Kellie, our idealistic five-year-old. "We could have a
pool, tennis courts, a basketball court for you, Dad, and a
big playhouse with lots of swings and slides. We could make
it just like a park and have all our friends over. Wouldn't
that be great?"

"Yeah," said Heather with a wide grin.

Don and I smiled at each other, enjoying the ima-
gination of our children, and for a few seconds we dreamed,
too. Who wouldn't love the opportunity to custom design
their own home? As I thought about the role architects play,
their awesome creativity struck me. A good architect can go
to a piece of barren property and envision the structure, the
landscape — even the internal floor plan. I would see nothing but weeds, dirt clods and litter.

THE ARCHITECT'S VISION

The intrigue about a good architect is evident in his
vision and creativity coupled with his structural expertise
and knowledge. Our builder friend John told me, "A good
architect will have building knowledge. If he and the builder
are two different people, they need to work closely together.
The builder is not a structural engineer, so he must depend

totally on what has been provided in the blueprints and specifications. If the architect has little actual building knowledge, he may not provide the detail needed by the builder for structural soundness."

"So," I said to John, "the ideal situation would be to have an architect who also does the building."

"That's exactly right. The best projects I have ever worked on are where the architect and builder are the same person or they do work closely together."

Never before had I understood the importance of the architect. I had just assumed he was a guy who came in, made a fancy drawing and charged an arm and a leg for being able to envision what the client could not see. After talking with John, I realized he was much more than that.

Then it hit me! Our God is our Architect as well as our Master Builder. He has provided the detailed specifications in His Word for building a marriage relationship. He has the vision and creativity to see our relationships in the fullness of what He intended them to be from the foundation of the world. He also has the "structural expertise" to know how our relationships need to be built.

What does our Architect envision for marriage relationships? If we think in terms of a house, it becomes clear that He desires a place of shelter, safety and security, a respite from the storms of life. Yet there is more to a "home" than that. It is a place for growth, bonding, nurturing, support, encouragement, accountability, companionship and intimacy. God's desire for marriage is a unity, a completion that takes place when a couple is joined together.

Obviously, God has a particular design in mind for marriage. Before we can address issues that result when victims marry, we must acquaint ourselves with God's specifications. He not only provides the architectural design, but He also promises to do the building. He gives us guidelines that will insure structural soundness, but He leaves room for us to have it "custom built."

He understands the components necessary for each couple's individual relationship. Our Master Architect/ Builder has produced blueprints for marriage so it will mirror the intimacy between Christ and the church.

EXAMINING THE BLUEPRINTS

Have you ever seen a set of blueprints? Recently John brought some over to our home. I was amazed. As I looked at the different sheets, it was like trying to read a foreign language. All the symbols, measurements and lines seemed to mesh together making it very hard to understand. However, John had no problem reading the blueprints — he is a contractor.

I recently spoke at a conference in San Diego, California. As always, I met several people who work behind the scenes in planning and preparation for such events. Darlene was one of them. She was in charge of overseeing the sound system. She was an organized woman, and she helped me set up my book table and "wired" me for sound. The morning session went well, and when time for lunch break came, Darlene asked if I had any plans. I said no so she invited me to join her. As we sat in the booth of a nearby restaurant getting acquainted, I told her about this book.

I said matter-of-factly, "It's been a really wonderful learning experience for me. I prayed for about six months, before the Lord put the outline on my heart. He impressed me to compare the marriage relationship to building a house. Since I knew nothing about building, I've had to be in close contact with contractors and others who've been through the construction process." Darlene seemed interested. Out of the blue, I switched the focus and asked, "Darlene, what do you do for a living?"

With a slight grin on her face, Darlene said, "I'm a licensed architect for the county of San Diego."

My mouth dropped. "Praise the Lord," I said, "I

couldn't have hoped for a better luncheon companion."

I proceeded to ask Darlene about her work, and I was fascinated with what she told me about blueprints.

"Blueprints are the designer's concept of the finished product. They provide a complete picture with all the details so the contractor can build. The blueprints don't tell the sequence of the process, only what it takes to build."

"I'm not quite sure I understand that," I said.

"Think of it this way," Darlene said, eyes sparkling. "Blueprints are like the ingredients in your favorite recipe. The contractor is the chef, who determines the sequence of putting those ingredients together. He provides the direction as to which ingredient is added at what point."

"You mean like the 'method' in a recipe?" I asked.

"That's right." Darlene went on to explain that a blueprint includes directions for many aspects of the project. There are architectural, mechanical, electrical, plumbing and structural blueprints and grading plans. These plans comprise civil blueprints, and they include soil report, topographical survey, elevations of land, etc. All these are designed to provide the specific measurements and specifications that will insure structural soundness.

I thought about how similar this was to God's Word. He provides the blueprint for every aspect of our lives. His Word is not limited only to explaining our relationship with Him, but also gives us details about living in the world and about building relationships with other people. He gives us a detailed blueprint so our "house" can meet His specifications for structural soundness. If, in the course of reading this book, you discover some needed repairs, seek the Master Builder for inspection and direction.

CLEAVING

What does it mean to "cleave" to your mate? In the Hebrew, the word *cleave* means to "glue" or "cling." It infers bonding together much like a strong adhesive. I think God purposely used this descriptive word to summon to our minds a vivid picture. If you've ever used Krazy glue or quick bonding glue like women use for nail repairs, you realize how very important it is to glue only what you intend to have bonded together. If you're like most of us, you have at one time or another inadvertently glued your finger or dripped some glue on an unintended surface. It is almost impossible to pull apart that which has bonded together. If it is your fingers, it is also painful.

God designed marriage to be the same way. He called us to bond or cleave together so tightly that we feel pain when we try to disengage. This does not mean we enmesh with each other and become each other's identity. We'll talk about the "one-flesh" relationship later in the chapter. It does mean that we come together and cling to each other on each level—body, soul and spirit.

We typically hear that the cleaving aspect of the marriage refers to physical bonding through the sexual relationship. This is only partly true. If cleaving does not take place on the other two levels, soul (emotional) and spirit, the relationship will show evidence of disrepair. Let's first examine spiritual bonding, as it is of primary importance for bonding to occur on the other two levels.

SPIRITUAL BONDING

What does it mean to be bonded spiritually to one another?

This concept became very clear to me one day when I attempted to install some plastic hooks on the back of our bathroom doors. I had seen some decorative hooks in the hardware store that I thought would look nice and provide extra space for towels. The hooks had adhesive on the back and came with detailed instructions showing how they were to be placed, along with a guarantee that they would hold a certain amount of weight.

The directions indicated that the surface on which the hook was to be placed needed to be clean, smooth and flat. I was anxious to get my hooks up, so I brushed the surface of the door with one swipe, peeled back the paper from the adhesive and pressed each hook into place. While swiping the door, I felt some slight ripples that looked like dirt that had been painted over. Because I had no intention of sanding that surface, I rationalized that those ripples, being ever so slight, "probably would not matter." I held the hooks in place for the prescribed time, pressing firmly as directed, and I delayed hanging any towels on them because the directions said to wait twenty-four hours. After bathing the girls the next day, I proudly hung the lightweight towels on the hooks. I was so pleased that I went out to the hardware store and purchased more hooks for our other bathroom.

A couple of days later it happened! I walked into the bathroom and found both towels on the floor along with the hooks. Attached to the adhesive on the back of the hooks were specks of dirt, hair and tiny paint particles. Clearly the hooks could not bear the weight of the towels because the adhesive had not bonded properly.

Unwilling to accept defeat, I purchased more hooks and glued them on the door. A week went by this time before the fated day came. I was frustrated, but I also realized that out of my enthusiasm I had failed to understand the importance of the clean, smooth surface in the bonding process.

As I reflected on this experience, I began to see the value of the lesson as it relates to marriage. For us to bond properly with our mates, we must remove all the debris. If we fail to continue scrubbing or sanding the surface clean throughout our marriage, the "weights" or trials of life which need support will cause our relationship to give way.

Being Equally Yoked

What does it mean to bond spiritually with your mate? First of all, the Scripture is very clear in 2 Corinthians

6:14 (NASB): "Do not be bound together with unbelievers; for what partnership have righteousness and lawlessness, or what fellowship has light with darkness?"

When we enter into a covenant relationship before God, He commands that both of us enter into that relationship having a personal commitment to Jesus Christ. Why is this so important? It is clear from this verse that trying to build a relationship with a nonbeliever is like trying to mesh or bring together totally opposing forces: righteousness and lawlessness, or light and darkness. In terms of building a house, it would be like trying to build one half of the house on solid, compacted soil and the other half on sand. The structure could not hold.

Does this mean that all who enter into an unequally yoked relationship are destined to have their marriage end in failure? Not at all, because where sin abounds, God's grace abounds even more. He gives us a guideline to insure the best possible result. He just wants us to know that when we step outside His guidelines, we will reap natural consequences for our actions.

As a teenager, I resisted this teaching on being unequally yoked. I was told by youth leaders to restrict my dating to Christian young men. The problem was, most of the Christian young men I knew were "duds." Few of them were vital Christians whom I could respect. I rationalized that I could date non-Christians and influence their lives by sharing Christ with them. How wrong I was. All too soon I would find myself compromising in small areas in my attempts to "win" them.

When I first met Don, he was not a believer. About five months into our dating relationship issues arose that indicated my walk with the Lord was again deteriorating. Through the counsel of a godly woman, and prayer, I realized I could not continue in the relationship. I felt hurt, but knew God was asking me to walk in obedience to Him, so I broke off our relationship. Don was crushed, but God had a greater plan in mind.

A man from Athletes in Action had challenged Don to a Bible study and through that Bible study, five months after we broke up, Don came to know Christ as his personal Savior. I now know God honored my obedience. How thankful I am that I got out of the way and allowed God's Spirit to work in Don's heart.

Don soon obtained another job that moved him out of the area. At first we didn't understand this, but later we realized that during those two years apart God solidified our spiritual walk for each of us. Don was discipled by two different men who were on staff with Campus Crusade for Christ, and he learned the basics of his faith and how to walk in newness of life.

Walking in Obedience and Harmony

God took me through two years of a "wilderness" experience. I was not dating, but I learned much about living happily as a single person. I was involved with other single young people in several Bible studies weekly, and my deep hunger for the Word of God developed out of that. God took what started as an unequally yoked relationship and caused us, individually, to learn the walk of obedience to Him before He brought us together in unity.

It is important to understand that being spiritually bonded together does not mean our relationships with the Lord will look exactly alike. Our individual relationship with the person of Jesus Christ will reflect individual differences. Think of your relationships with others, especially with your children, if you have them. Your relationship with each child is unique. It is reflective of the uniqueness of your character as well as the character of the child with whom you are relating. So it is with God.

During our premarital counseling I became concerned that I had been a Christian much longer than Don and that our religious backgrounds and training were so dissimilar. We varied in the way we prayed, worshiped, and had our devotional time. I went with these concerns to the pastor who was to marry us, and he gave me some very sound advice.

He said, "Don't focus on the differences. It is clear that both of you believe in the Lord Jesus and that you seek to have Him as the center of your home and relationship. Don't make these other things an issue, Jan, but choose to love, honor and respect Don's relationship with the Lord as separate from yours."

The mutual respect we have for our individual relationships with our Lord has proven over the years to bond us together. I see many couples who struggle in this area. They often make the mistake of harping on differences, which undermines their relationship, rather than trusting God to work in the heart of their mate. Certainly there are vital, uncompromisable doctrinal issues which must be agreed upon if marital harmony is achieved. However, there are other aspects, characteristics and even some doctrines in which we may differ that should not be allowed to become focal points.

The spiritual bonding that exists between a man and a woman in marriage is intended to mirror Christ's relationship with the church. We read in Ephesians 5:32 that Paul refers to the marital bond as a "great mystery," likened to Christ and the church. As I think about Christ's relationship with His body, three characteristics seem of utmost importance: covenant (spirit), commitment (soul/emotional), and communion (body/physical).

Covenant (Spirit)

What does it mean to be in a covenant relationship? According to Webster's Dictionary, *covenant* means a "binding agreement; a written agreement or promise usually under seal between two or more parties." When we enter into a marriage we are in covenant with our mate before

God. It was designed to be a binding agreement.

I believe God regards the covenants we enter into seriously. Ecclesiastes 5:4,5 (NIV) says:

> When you make a vow to God, do not delay in fulfilling it. He has no pleasure in fools; fulfill your vow. It is better not to vow than to make a vow and not fulfill it.

We see from other Scriptures that the only circumstance that nullifies a covenant agreement is death. That is why our marriage vows include the phrase "until death do us part." Unfortunately, marriage seems to be entered into these days with a clause in fine print that says "until death do us part, or until I change my mind."

If a couple has truly entered into a covenant relationship with each other, they have agreed before God to an exclusive commitment one to the other, to be broken only by death. When Don and I took our vows we spent time together, committing to each other that no matter what was around the corner, divorce was not an option. Each of our daughters has become increasingly more inquisitive about divorce as they encounter friends at school or relatives who experience breakups. On several occasions we have reaffirmed our vows before them. We have told them that Jesus made marriage to last a lifetime and that we have made a vow to spend the rest of our lives together. This is only possible as we remain connected to God through cultivating our relationship with Jesus Christ. In John 15:5*b* Jesus said, "Without Me you can do nothing."

I recognize that many who might be reading have already experienced the trauma of a marriage breakup. I know that many times circumstances are truly beyond our control and it has resulted in divorce. Other times, divorce has been sought after a clear violation of the covenant relationship as outlined in the Scripture. In these cases, and others, I urge persons to receive in full the love, mercy and grace of our Lord Jesus, and I admonish them to examine themselves and their prospective mates carefully before entering into the marital bond again.

In Song of Solomon, the book that beautifully describes marital love, we read:

> Set me as a seal upon thine heart, as a seal upon thine arm: for love is strong as death ... Many waters cannot quench love, neither can the floods drown it (8:6*a* and 7*a*, KJV).

Jesus has entered into a spiritual covenant relationship with all who have accepted Him as their Savior and Lord. This is a binding agreement "with whom you were sealed for the day of redemption" according to Ephesians 4:30*b* (NIV). We are to model that kind of covenant relationship with our mates. It is upon the foundation of the covenant that our commitment is established and formed.

Commitment (Soul/Emotional)

How does commitment to our marriage or to our relationship with the Lord differ from that of covenant? It may be helpful to look at the covenant aspect of the relationship as the binding agreement between spouses, between a person and his God, and between God and His children. Commitment seems to involve something more.

What comes to your mind when you hear someone say, that woman is really committed to her husband? Or that man is committed to his family? Or that athlete is committed to the game? Does commitment only mean that you put something or someone in a position of priority? Or is there a part of commitment that implies active involvement, a dedicated determination?

After asking myself these questions and observing other marriages, I have concluded that, to me, commitment speaks of action, action stimulated by a strong belief.

Commitment is the covenant in action.

When commitment is limited to putting something

or someone in a position of priority without a purposeful plan of action, it is subject to stagnation and mediocrity. I know a couple whose marriage has lasted forty-six years. They have considerable commitment to their relationship on the basis of years together. Yet if you could look behind their closed doors, you would find they have not shared a bed nor a bedroom for more than ten years. They eat meals separately, have very little meaningful conversation, go few places together other than occasional family functions, have no couple friends their own age, take separate vacations, and have not expressed or demonstrated affection as long as they can remember. Is this commitment to a marriage or apathy shrouded in the security of the known?

Don and I talked over this element of commitment, and he matter-of-factly said, "It's more than just putting in time — like clocking in and out. You 'put in time' in prison because you're 'committed.' Hopefully, the commitment in marriage is more than just putting in time!"

I know for some, marriage does at times seem like prison. Most of us who are married can recall those years prior to marriage when you could just make plans to go play golf or go shopping without having to "check with your mate." Those periods of our single life appeal to our more selfish nature, yet God designed marriage to be fulfilling and rewarding. If we are committed, actively pursuing a purposeful plan toward oneness, we will experience the realization of His promises.

What does commitment involve?

Since Don has coached basketball for twenty years, I have been around a lot of players. I have learned the lingo, suffered through the losses, rejoiced at the victories, and become accustomed to the game and what it takes to play. I often ask Don questions about basketball — about the players, the coaches, different aspects of the game. It is not strange that much of what he shares about playing basketball and being an athlete is applicable to life in general. In the Scriptures Paul even used the analogy of the athlete when in 1 Corinthians 9:24-27 he says:

> Do you not know that in a race all the runners run, but only one gets the prize? Run in such a way as to get the prize. Everyone who competes in the games goes into strict training. They do it to get a crown that will not last; but we do it to get a crown that will last forever. Therefore I do not run like a man running aimlessly; I do not fight like a man beating the air. No, I beat my body and make it my slave so that after I have preached to others, I myself will not be disqualified for the prize (NIV).

I asked Don, "What does it mean when you describe one of your players as being 'committed to the game'?"

He replied, "It's a player who's willing to do the things required of him to make him as good as he can be. It's a guy who works on his game even when the coach is not around. He goes beyond what is expected because he desires to be the best he can be."

"What all does that involve?" I asked.

"He trains. He works on his weaknesses, hones his strengths, does all that he can to improve and keep improving. He prepares himself for competition. He prepares for the game mentally as well as physically."

Don looked thoughtfully at me and then he added, "All those things he does for himself. The final two characteristics of a fine, committed athlete are that he is committed to the team and he is teachable. He is willing to make plays to help the team, even if it means personal sacrifice. A team player is hard to find. The ones with a teachable attitude we call coachable. They are a cut above the rest. They don't have an 'I know it all' attitude, and they allow the coach to instruct them. These are the guys you can count on in the gut of the game—they'll come through for you with all they've got."

Couples committed to marriage are like the athlete

committed to the team. Each spouse works to become the best he or she can be. They acquaint themselves with their own weaknesses, enhance their strengths, develop a mind-set for doing their part in strengthening the marriage, and are amenable to learning from their mate, as well as from God, about ways in which they can improve. They work for the good of the team.

Remember, commitment is the covenant in action. It is an investment of time, but more important, an investment of yourself — spirit, soul (emotional) and body.

Communion (Body/Physical)

We have talked about the importance of severance and cleaving. It should be clarified that both of these principles as outlined by God are prerequisites for the coming together as "one flesh." The oneness that takes place in a marriage must be a continual process. It can be nurtured — or neglected.

What does it mean to be "one flesh"? As a single person listening to sermons on marriage, I tended to visualize the "one-flesh" relationship in a single dimension: the physical. For a long time I thought this term was a nice way to talk about the intimacy of the sexual relationship between marriage partners. After marrying, I discovered through experience the broader sense of what that oneness is.

In *Strike the Original Match* Chuck Swindoll writes:

> Becoming one flesh suggests a process, not an instant fact. Two people with different backgrounds, temperaments, habits, scars, feelings, parents, educational pursuits, gifts and interests don't immediately leave a wedding ceremony in perfect unity. The process begins there.[1]

Like severance and cleaving, the one-flesh relationship was designed by God to exist on all three levels: body, soul and spirit. It is a coming together in unity, or a communion on each of those levels.

The simplest way to look at being in communion is to understand the Greek word *koinonia*, as it is used in the New Testament. The word means being in "fellowship" or "partnership." If we are to develop a one-flesh relationship, we will of necessity have to be in fellowship with our mates in the spiritual, emotional and physical realms.

How is fellowship developed? Don and I recently were asked to join a prayer group. The initial goal of the group was to support, through prayer, another couple in our Sunday school class who were experiencing great trials. The Wilsons are committed believers who seemed to be under tremendous attack, some of which we felt was due to their ministry to certain cults. The prayer group was limited to the Wilsons, for whom we were praying, the host couple, the Gebhards, ourselves, and two other couples. Although all of us had been acquainted prior to our first prayer meeting, none had developed a close relationship with any others.

As weeks passed, the barriers began to break down. At first we prayed for the Wilsons' needs. Then we began praying for each other's general needs. Finally we began to confess to each other some individual personal needs. Now we experience a growing depth of love for one another. How did this happen?

Time, Trust and Prayer

First, to grow, all relationships need *time*. The element of time allows for key components in relationships to be established. You cannot know someone without spending time with them.

Trust, which comes after knowing, is also a major component in a relationship. You have probably heard the phrase, you cannot trust someone you do not know. Jesus fully understood the need of the human heart, so He spent hours and days with His disciples fostering a relationship of trust. We see evidence of Jesus acknowledging time as an important element of trust in a relationship in John 14. In verses 6 and 7 Jesus talks to His disciples about His relationship with the Father.

In verse 8 Philip asked, "Lord, show us the Father, and it is sufficient for us."

Jesus answered, "Have I been with you so long, and yet you have not known Me, Philip? He who has seen Me has seen the Father; so how can you say, 'Show us the Father'?"

Spending time with our mates is one way to foster trust and to develop the one-flesh relationship.

What other element helped in drawing our prayer group together? *Sharing our hearts* with one another. I like the word *communing,* although we hear it very little today. According to Webster's dictionary, it means to "communicate intimately." When we had spent enough time together to establish a trust and respect for each other, it was safe to begin sharing on a deeper level.

In the beginning of Don's and my relationship, he did not understand all the intricacies of what it meant to be married to someone who had been sexually abused. At times, it was very difficult for him to understand why all of the hurt from my past could not simply be forgotten. Even during those confusing times, though, he remained open to hearing my pain without judgment or minimizing its importance. He did not handle everything perfectly, but for the most part, I knew he loved me unconditionally and that I could trust him with the things that mattered to me.

What final element was the catalyst in building our prayer group?

Prayer. There is no better way to create spiritual unity in a marriage than to pray. It seems for us that when we pray together, it is practically impossible for any walls to remain between us. Even if the particular issue we are praying over does not immediately resolve itself, praying about it, confessing our individual sins and weaknesses, and expressing our desire for God to have His way in our lives all bring us into a unity in spirit.

It is very difficult for me to hide my feelings from the Lord, and so, when Don and I pray together, we share a special kind of intimacy. When we lower our defenses and allow ourselves to be seen by others, closeness develops.

We have talked about how spending time with one another, communicating intimately, and praying all help to foster the one-flesh relationship. As we look at these more closely, we see that each is representative of the three levels previously mentioned — physical, emotional and spiritual. Spending time together requires a physical commitment. Communicating intimately taps into the emotional realm of the relationship which adds depth and closeness. Finally, prayer helps us to realize the limits of our human resources and gives us time to summon the strength that we need from our God.

We know now that God does have a divine blueprint in mind for marriage. We have looked at what it means to cleave to our mate and what it is to be in a covenant relationship, and we have seen that true commitment is covenant in action. We have discussed the one-flesh relationship and how it can be fostered through communing on the physical, emotional and spiritual levels.

I have purposely not discussed sexual intimacy — we will address that issue in detail later.

We are now ready to understand better what elements complicate proper bonding with our mate and prevent our establishing a sound foundation in marriage. In every construction project, periodic inspections are scheduled at regular intervals before the building continues. Let's examine some of the areas you may need to inspect prior to moving ahead.

4

Periodic Inspections

I have friends who, in the process of remodeling their home, are adding 800 square feet to their upstairs floor. The work began last December and has gone on for nine months. In many ways, it has been a nightmare.

They live in a planned community here in Southern California, so from the beginning, they had to submit their building plans not only to the city but also to their local community association for approval. These organizations look over the plans of every proposed construction in their area to insure structural soundness, to make certain the plans adhere to city standards and specifications, and to guarantee aesthetic harmony within the surrounding community.

After plans have been approved and construction begun, periodic inspections must be made throughout the process. Soil must be inspected for proper compaction; reinforcing steel bars (sometimes called collectively, "re-bar") must be checked before the foundation is poured; the slab has to be examined for proper utility installation; and the framing must be approved prior to hanging the drywall.

At each step, a city inspector evaluates whether or not the work is up to standard. If it is, it may proceed. If not, corrections must be made. At each point it must be signed off before construction can get under way again. Sometimes work is delayed for a day, other times it can take a week. In rare cases, if the builder has not met the specifications, the city may prohibit any more work on the project until the builder tears the whole thing apart and starts again from scratch.

It's too bad a similar system is not employed in a marriage relationship. How helpful it might be to have periodic inspections to insure our relationship is headed in the right direction. Instead, most of us get married and carry on our relationship for years without ever probing into its construction. Usually a short develops in the electrical wiring or a major plumbing problem arises before we see the need to correct damage that has been behind the walls for years. When victims marry, they definitely need periodic inspections along the way as well as initial inspections.

INSPECTION QUESTIONS

We have used the following questions to initiate conversation and exploration as you make your periodic inspections. Take time to sit down privately and answer the questions. Then sit down with your mate or prospective mate and go on an expedition together. Your talking probably will stimulate more questions. Share your feelings as much as possible. Have your partner reflect back to you what he (or she) has heard you say. Finally, discuss ways you can compromise and come to a better understanding about how you both want these areas in your relationship changed or improved. Be specific and set some goals.

Dealing With Conflict:

- How did your parents deal with conflict?
- When conflict arose in your family, what happened

(silence, withdrawal, explosive anger, open discussion, etc.)?

- How was conflict resolved?
- Did one parent always seem to "win in the end"?

Parenting:

- How was love demonstrated in your family of origin?
- How were you disciplined?
- Was the discipline harsh or suited to the offense?
- Did you live up to your parents' expectations?

Finances:

- How did you learn about money management?
- Who took primary responsibility for money matters in your home? What significant patterns do you have today that reflect your family's view of finances?
- What was your family's philosophy or motto regarding money (not what was said, but what was lived)?

Sex:

- Was appropriate physical affection shown in your family?
- Was sex a taboo subject?
- How were nudity and sexual issues handled?
- What was the underlying tone in your home regarding sex and your sexuality?

Communication:

- Was it safe to talk about feelings?
- Who was the communicator in your family?
- Were you expected to "read minds"?
- Could you express your emotional needs and receive a proper response?

In-Laws/Extended Family:

- What role did your grandparents play in your family?
- Was family loyalty important?
- Were there family secrets that were forbidden subjects?
- Who, besides your parents, could you go to for support and understanding?

Recreation:

- Was having fun as a family "legislated" in your home?
- Did you vacation as a family?
- Was it an enjoyable experience?
- What family activities stand out in your mind?
- Was recreation a leisurely experience or just another arena for competitiveness?

Spiritual:

- How was God's character portrayed in your family?
- Was tradition more important than true relationship with God?
- What one significant message about yourself and about God did you come out of childhood believing?
- Do you *feel* a true sense of God's acceptance and love?

As you pondered and discussed these questions, you may have been as surprised, as we were, about some of the similarities and some of the differences you share. Let's look at each of these areas in more depth now.

DEALING WITH CONFLICT

Don grew up in a home where conflict was avoided. When it did arise, his mother did not deal with it directly and his father went into withdrawal. Don remembers his parents having late night arguments with little resolution ever resulting. His father's withdrawal episodes would last for days. He would sit for hours at a time in his chair puffing away on cigarette after cigarette, refusing to engage in conversation even at meals. All the kids knew not to approach Dad until he made the first move. Eventually, he would emerge from his self-induced solitary confinement as if nothing had happened.

I grew up in a home where conflict was vocally explosive, or my mother diverted it through planned manipulation. Most of the conflicts my parents had seemed to center around money or dealing with us kids. When my parents disagreed over something that pertained to us, they often yelled and screamed, and it would end with my mother coming to us and saying, "You know how your dad is. He's not going to change, so you'll just have to learn to adjust."

My mother played the mediator/manipulator. We learned to approach her on "delicate" issues and she would instruct us when and how much to tell Dad. We learned how to manipulate the situation to our own advantage by waiting for the "appropriate" time to ask our requests, such as after Dad had his first drink of the evening. We learned to read his moods and scope out the situation.

Conflicts were rarely openly discussed. If my dad ever lost a conflict, he would brood for days having little or no contact with any of us. We knew to stay clear as he sat like a statue in his Lazy Boy recliner, stoically watching T.V., disconnected from all around him. My mother did not dare venture into his world of isolation, but patiently waited for his re-entry into our world.

It's no wonder that when Don and I married we experienced some difficulty in the area of conflict. Don had picked up his mother's pattern of avoiding conflict at all cost; I would avoid the conflict by pouting sometimes for days, often utilizing manipulative hints or innuendos to make Don aware of my hurt, or reach a point of frustration and explode in anger. We both began to realize that these patterns were causing us to feel distant, resentful and bitter. That was the first step in beginning to change. We sometimes still catch ourselves in those old patterns! In a later chapter we will discuss some practical ways we've tried to change in this area.

PARENTING

As we examined the area of parenting, we found that both sets of our parents exemplified many good things. Both emphasized a respect for those in authority, a desire to excel and be a hard worker, and the need for discipline. Unfortunately, in Don's home there was little, if any, physical affection shown. Early in our marriage Don and I discussed how love was demonstrated in his home, and he matter-of-factly said, "I can't ever remember either of my parents telling me they loved me when I was growing up." I was aghast. Don was past thirty before he heard those words from his parents.

Physical affection was shown in my home, but it was often accompanied with an undercurrent of perversion, due to previous molestation incidents. As a child, I felt a great hunger for physical affection, but I also often felt a lingering distrust about where it might lead. This greatly impacted our marriage relationship! Don came into marriage starved for the love and affection he had been deprived of, and I came into it with all types of fear and distrust that made me want to avoid physical contact, while hungering desperately for appropriate love and affection. It has taken years for us to work through these issues, and we will discuss them at length in the "plumbing" chapter.

Discipline in my home was, more often than not, harsh and irrelevant to the offense at hand. I grew up in such an extremely rigid system that I was forbidden even to go to a public library until I was sixteen. My stepfather maintained an iron hand and my mother backed up his rigid standards and demands.

One of the most eye-opening realizations about discipline in our home came to me recently as I was struggling over an issue in my walk with the Lord. When I would sin or "fail" the Lord in some way, I would walk around for days unable to accept God's forgiveness. I knew in my mind that I was forgiven, but I still felt I had to hang my head in shame for days.

One day, after the Holy Spirit convicted me of a sinful pattern in my life, I went into a deep despair for about two days, unable even to talk to the Lord. On the third day, I asked the Lord what was wrong with me and why it was so difficult for me to forgive myself. The Holy Spirit impressed me clearly with a profound realization about my childhood. He seemed to say, *Jan, when you were disciplined as a child, the discipline was never over — even when it was over.*

As I thought about this, I realized it was true. Discipline was handled in such a way that it induced shame and guilt. Even after a spanking, or coming out of my room after being punished, I was expected to hang my head and not smile. If I exhibited any sign of a lack of remorse, I was punished further.

What an insight! God began to heal me right then as He gave me that awareness. He unmistakably showed me that His discipline for His children is from a loving, joyful heart and that His Son Jesus already bore the shame. He freed me from having to bear that shame myself.

This understanding has helped greatly as I discipline my own girls. I consciously have attempted to change the shame-based approach. I hug my girls after their transgressions, reaffirming my love and God's love for them, and I say to them, "It's over. You've admitted you were wrong and have accepted the discipline, so it's done. It's gone because

Jesus promised to 'cleanse us from all unrighteousness.' "

FINANCES

Don and I definitely grew up with different views when it comes to finances!

He grew up in a family with seven children. Although his family was not poor, their resources were limited. Don tends to be conservative, a saver, and he does not like to buy on credit.

I grew up in the lower middle-class, yet we always seemed to have a lovely home with the most modern conveniences. My parents used credit and often overextended. As a young adult, my Mastercard was always used up to the limit. I went into marriage believing that as long as there were checks in the checkbook, there was money in the bank.

These differences in our backgrounds have fueled the fire of many financial "discussions" through the last ten years of marriage.

We have had to come to several agreements. When we first married Don instituted the "no Mastercard policy." With the exception of a few emergencies and a few extravagances, we have maintained this policy and it has proven to be a wise choice.

Because of my temperament, it is important to me to "see" the fruit of my labor. When we received our first royalty check of $1,000, I envisioned a new refrigerator. Don, on the other hand, envisioned a "cushion" in the savings account. I had all the logical reasons behind my purchase: Our other refrigerator was ten years old because I had purchased it when I was still single; it was only 15 cubic feet, hardly large enough for a family of four; it really did not fit our almond-colored kitchen; and, "I really deserve this for all my hard work."

Don was thinking more logically in terms of money we needed for the summer, having a little extra on hand for unforseen emergencies, and just simply having money in the savings account.

We ended up compromising. I didn't get the refrigerator, but I was able to buy a few items for the house, and we did put some of the money away in savings.

Finances are a difficult area for couples no matter how much money they have. I know many wealthy couples, and many couples who are barely making it, who both struggle in managing their finances. It is healthy to examine your background in this area and to make periodic inspections to assess where you have been and where you are going.

SEX

About five years into our marriage, Don and I talked about how we would instruct our two little girls in the area of their sexuality. During that discussion we each shared how we learned about the intimacy of marriage. Don's parents never sat down with him to discuss his entry into puberty; he mainly depended on "hearing it from the guys." He did say they had films in their junior high school, but he never could figure out the anatomical diagrams!

I shared with him, rather matter-of-factly, that as part of my sex education as a 5th or 6th grader I was made to watch my parents engage in sexual intercourse.

As soon as the words came out of my mouth, Don gasped and said, "Honey, that was sick!"

His words set me back for a moment. I said, "You're right; it was. But you see, for me it was normal. It was all I knew."

Having my own children has made me realize how perverted some of what I grew up seeing and experiencing really was.

Some things that might seem relatively harmless need to be assessed. Nudity in the home is one of these. A friend of mine in graduate school did a research paper on nudity in the home. She found that, basically, the extremes were the danger zones. Too much nudity, in the name of "openness," can be detrimental to the healthy development of a child's sexuality. It may even be a form of sexual exploitation. On the other hand, nudity that is seen as "shameful" can leave a child feeling self-hatred for themselves and their bodies. Because of the perversion in my own home, and the lack of good modeling in Don's, we sought wisdom from others on these issues. A psychologist friend of ours, when asked about nudity around children, said that when children reach age five, a parent, particularly of the opposite sex, needs to begin to be more modest. We have attempted to create a balance in this area for our girls.

In the "plumbing check" chapter we will discuss, in more detail, how the sexual relationship is affected by dysfunction in some of these areas.

COMMUNICATION

We have already shared a little of our backgrounds with regard to communication. Don grew up in a family where feelings were not identified, expressed or acknowledged. This, of course, has had a significant impact on our marital relationship. Don has spent considerable time personally working on being a better communicator. We get ourselves into trouble when we are not honest or clear with each other about what we really feel or want.

I grew up in a home where it was not safe to ask for your needs to be met, so I learned to manipulate and communicate indirectly. Early in our marriage, I struggled with these issues. I'll never forget one day when we were on our way home after spending all day at the beach. I really was in no mood to cook and I realized our favorite pizza spot was somewhat on the way home. The conversation went something like this:

"Boy, I sure am hungry," I said.

"Yeah, me too," Don answered.

(Approaching the turn we would make to go to the restaurant) "Gosh, I don't think I have a thing in the refrigerator to eat."

Don: (no comment).

(A block from the turn) "Well, there's the street we'd turn on if we were going to Mamma Cozza's."

"Yep, there it is."

Don was unaware of my hidden agenda, so he drove on past.

The closer we got to home, the angrier I became. Why was Don not catching on?

We finally arrived home. I opened the refrigerator and angrily said, "I knew it. There's nothing in here to eat." I started opening all the cupboards, then slamming them shut. It didn't take long for Don to notice.

"What's wrong with you?"

"I'm mad!"

"What about?" he asked innocently.

"I wanted to go to Mamma Cozza's for dinner and YOU wouldn't take me!"

Don looked totally lost. He simply said, "Jan, you never asked me. I could have gone for pizza myself tonight."

I realized then that, in the past, it had not been okay to ask for things in my family. Instead, I had learned a deceptive type of communication pattern that kept me from the pain of rejection but I often also became frustrated over not having my needs met.

Don grew up with such denial, due to his father's alcoholism, that he learned to tune out. He shut his feelings off and to this day has difficulty knowing what he is feeling.

Some of you men may be saying, "What's the big deal, all this stuff about feelings?"

Well, this area is critical in your sexual relationship with your wife. We'll explain why when we get into the "plumbing" chapter.

IN-LAWS/EXTENDED FAMILY

Don had little contact with his grandparents while he was growing up. Most of the support he recalls receiving as a young boy came from his Little League coach. During Don's teenage years, one of his high school basketball coaches was particularly influential. Don reflects on that time now and says most of his support in life came through his athletic relationships and accomplishments.

Although I did not have a great deal of contact with my grandparents, the contact I did have was positive. My maternal grandparents were very old, but we still spent time at their home. Grandma Garrett was the "preacher" I spoke of earlier in the book, and her prayers and modeling were deeply imprinted upon my heart. My stepgrandfather also played a significant role in my life. We only saw him and my stepgrandmother a few times, but Grandpa was a godly man who would sit down with me, open his Bible and share from his heart. As a teenager, I received from him valuable advice that helped me learn to walk in obedience to God and trust Him for results in later years.

Two other families provided tremendous support for me when I was a teen. One was the family of my best friend, Lauren Littauer. I worked in their family restaurant and spent considerable time in their home.

The other family lived next door to us. I babysat for their two boys. The Lancasters, in their thirties, exemplified to me an ideal marriage. I remember praying as a teenager that God would give me a man like Jim Lancaster and make my relationship as tender as Jim and Pat's. I spent hours at their house, confiding in them and soaking up their love.

RECREATION

Don loves to travel. Since his dad was a Naval officer, Don spent a lot of time traveling when he was a young boy. (The highlight was living in Japan.) Don still loves planning trips and seeing the sights.

I am less than an ideal traveler. We did a great deal of camping when I was a child, but, although we saw a lot of the U.S., traveling often was not a pleasant experience for me. My stepdad would try to "legislate" fun. He demanded so much on the trips that the joy of family life was lost. For example, we couldn't sleep while traveling by car because we had to "enjoy the scenery."

Early in our marriage, I seemed to be plagued constantly by migraine headaches. Don noticed that these headaches often came on when we were traveling. This was particularly hard on Don because he enjoyed getting away so much. It seemed like I was sabotaging our time together. After he made that observation, I began to work through some of the emotions I felt as a child, and since then I have been able to take pleasure in family outings.

SPIRITUAL

I am thankful that, amidst all the dysfunction in my home, worshiping God as a family held a high priority.

Even as a young child, I had a hunger for God's Word. As I got older, it became difficult to live with the hypocrisy displayed by my parents, but the positive aspect of this was that I knew I must live out what I said I believed. What I saw exhibited in my home made me want to be an authentic Christian.

Unfortunately, the first fifteen years of my walk with God was rooted in a performance mentality. It has been only as God has healed the wounds of my past that I have been able to recognize God's absolute gift of love with no strings attached. He has had to do much repair work in bringing my distorted image of myself and of Him into alignment with His Word.

Don's family had always encouraged him to attend church and to be active in it. He grew up believing there was a God, but he never knew until adulthood that he could have a personal relationship with Him. He had transfered the image of his father's harsh temperament to God. To Don, God was not approachable and Don was unacceptable. When he became an adult, Don finally did become a Christian. Even then, because of their loyalty to their church and denomination, an underlying ripple of betrayal ran through Don's family—Don was attending a fundamental, Bible-teaching church!

As God has continued to heal both of us of childhood hurts, we have entered into a deeper love for each other through grasping the depth of the Savior's personal love for both of us.

The questions given earlier focus primarily on your foundations, laid in your family of origin. The list is meant to be a springboard from there to future communication, to help you recognize issues of your past and understand how they shape your present attitudes and behavior.

Since, realistically, no one will scrutinize your marriage relationship like the city inspector does a construction project, it is vital that you and your mate schedule "periodic inspections" to protect the building of your relationship. Remember, the purpose of the inspection is to make sure the construction is up to specifications. If it is not, don't try to skip over the problem to proceed with the building. Instead, seek help in correcting the problem so that the structure, your marriage relationship, will hold firm.

5

Plumbing Check

When we moved into our house a little over five years ago, I was thrilled. The house was about eighteen years old and was in a nice neighborhood, not far from schools or our church. I was glad to get into an older home because it had some features not obtainable in the newer homes that we could afford, things like porcelain bathtubs and sinks, tiled kitchen counters and showers, and a larger yard.

It is often hard to know about the condition of certain things in a home, like plumbing, until you're faced with the repair. Sometimes you are forewarned, but you may not heed the warning signals or even recognize them.

A little over a year ago, while cleaning the cupboard under our bathroom sink one day, I observed a few water stains on some of the items. I looked at the pipes but did not see any water dripping although I did feel some dampness. I told Don about the slight leak, saying we may need to get it looked at. It was at the height of basketball season and it must have slipped his mind.

I thought nothing more about it, either, for a few weeks, until one evening about 10 P.M. when I went into the bathroom to get ready for bed. Don was not home yet from his game. When I turned on the water to wash my face, I heard a hissing sound. At first, I couldn't figure out what it was. I looked out the bathroom window to see if someone had turned on a sprinkler. That wasn't it.

Then I remembered the leak. I opened the cupboard—everything was drenched and about a quarter inch of water stood in the back of the cupboard! I had started removing everything when Don walked in.

"What's happened?" he asked.

"Remember that little leak I told you about a few weeks ago? It's now turned into a major one."

Don turned off the valves under the sink and all seemed fine. He went into the other bathroom. The month-old carpet squished with each step.

"Jan," Don called, "I think we have a problem."

Most plumbing problems occur on the weekends—this was Saturday night. We didn't know what to do next; we thought maybe there was a main-line break. I called a 24-hour plumber's answering service. The plumber called back and instructed us to turn off the main water valve outside until we could determine what had happened. He could come out some time on Sunday, but it would be at "time-and-a-half."

I mopped up the water in our bathroom cupboard and Don and I ripped up the new carpet in the other bathroom and discovered the pad was completely soaked. We went to bed that evening, not sure what we were facing.

I called the plumber on Sunday. He told me how to test whether it was a main-line break or whether the water from the one bathroom had just gone under the wall into the other bath.

Gratefully, we found out it was not a main-line break, just a pipe in our bathroom that had gone from a drip to a flow. We scheduled to have the plumber come out on Monday morning.

We called our carpet layer, a personal friend, and he came out that morning. "Fortunately," he said, "you pulled the carpet up in time and all you need to replace is the pad."

When the plumber came Monday morning, he found a hole in one of the pipes and said it must have been dripping for weeks to cause that much flooding. We were lucky it wasn't a main-line break. "What would have happened if it were?" I asked, somewhat relieved.

"Well, first, you'd have had to determine where it was. Then if it were somewhere under your house, you'd have to break up the cement slab to repair it."

"You mean there's no way to crawl under somewhere to get to the plumbing lines?" I asked naively.

"Not in your home," he said. "This is a cement slab." He pointed to an area in our garage that leads into the kitchen. "The only way to get to the main line is to go through the cement slab. It's expensive and messy."

Suddenly, I was even more thankful for the pipe in the bathroom. I asked the plumber to look at the other pipes to make sure they were in good shape. He did the job and handed me the bill.

I thought to myself, *Next time there's even a slight problem, I'm calling someone. I sure don't want that to happen again!*

RECOGNIZING THERE IS A PROBLEM

Sometimes in our relationships, we see signs of a potential problem, but we do not respond immediately. Problems rarely just take care of themselves, but somehow we like to think they will. I saw the water spots in the cupboard, but thought it was not a problem that needed immediate attention. I was wrong.

When Don and I talked about that plumbing problem a year later, he said, "You know, there's nothing more annoying in a house than having a plumbing problem."

Then he added, "For a man, there's nothing more annoying in a marriage than having a sexual problem."

When Don and I married, we loved each other; we were physically attracted to each other, and we thought that was all it took to have a fulfilling sexual relationship. Neither of us realized that, when victims marry, sexual problems threaten every aspect of their relationship. As with that pipe in the bathroom, erosion that leads to a major problem does not happen overnight. The pipe had been eroding for some time before the dripping began. In the same way, the events of both of our pasts had been eroding our lives in ways that were not easy to recognize.

What does being a victim have to do with the sexual relationship? Why are there problems in this area so often?

When we married, Don and I seemed to have a good sexual relationship, yet he commented early in our marriage that during those intimate times I seemed far away. I shrugged his comments off and said we were still in the process of getting to know each other

I did notice a change in my attitude toward sex, but thought it was just that "the honeymoon was over." I really had no desire for sex most of the time. I wanted closeness, but I did not especially want to engage in intercourse to have that closeness.

When I told Don I felt I needed counseling to help me resolve the issues from my past, our sexual relationship seemed even worse.

During the process of the therapy, my sexual desire seemed almost non-existent. Every time Don touched me, I reacted negatively. If he would come home from work and pat me as he passed by, internally I would cringe. It seemed all Don was interested in was sex.

Don couldn't understand what was happening. I seemed to be pulling further and further away. Why? Was it something about him?

IN THE MIND OF AN ABUSE VICTIM

When someone has been a victim of sexual abuse, it is often difficult to separate the past from the present. Though I clearly understood what had happened in my past, certain things in the present sometimes still triggered unpleasant memories and emotions. It was similar to what happens to Vietnam veterans. The technical term is post-traumatic stress disorder. A present event becomes the stimulus that triggers a flashback. It can be anything. For me, it was the way Don touched me at times, or a sound he made when we were being intimate, or his attempts to embrace me when I was sleeping. All of these could flash me back into my childhood bedroom where I would relive a segment of the abuse I endured as a child.

It was a frightening experience, one that Don did not understand at first. It hit home one night about three years into our marriage. As Don tells it, he was wanting to be intimate with me, so he showered, put on some aftershave, did a few pushups and prepared for bed. We went to bed and began caressing. All of a sudden I froze. My entire body became stiff as a board. I couldn't move. I felt strange. It was like I was there in bed with my husband, but I wasn't there. I knew enough from being in therapy to know something had triggered this flashback. Don and I talked for a few minutes and ruled out several possibilities. It wasn't the way he touched me; it wasn't the lighting in the room; it wasn't anything obvious. As I lay there, Don just held me close. The trigger suddenly became clear as I nestled to my husband's chest. He had put on the very same aftershave my stepfather had worn for years. My memory made the connection before I knew what was happening.

The victim of sexual abuse begins to believe many lies about herself as a result of the abuse. Some of those lies are centered around her value as a person. The victim often feels her only value is determined by her sexuality. Many victims find themselves sexually active prior to marriage, only to marry and then have little desire for sexual intimacy with their mate. Some of this is due to faulty thinking.

My stepdad had told me as I was growing up that young men were interested in me for only "one thing." The underlying message I received was that only my "body" had any value. When I married, I desperately wanted Don to love ME, separate from sex. Unfortunately, the only way to gain proof that he really loved ME was to stop engaging in sex to test his love. Don had no idea of my thoughts, nor did he enter into marriage to be celibate. We have had to work through this erroneous thinking through the years. It has taken time for me to really believe Don loves ME. I have had to understand it is possible for me to feel that love without withdrawing sexually.

I do believe there will be times in the healing process when a victim may need to have some space and to be given a choice about participating in sexual intimacy. In his chapter to husbands, "Is the Roof Leaking?" Don will share some practical ways to help in this area.

IT TAKES TWO

For the first six years of our marriage, I assumed that all the difficulties we had in our sexual relationship were due to my being a victim of sexual abuse. Don had no trouble performing, so it was all too clear who had the problem.

After writing *A Door of Hope,* I went back to school to get my master's degree in marriage, family and child counseling. That program requires each student to obtain at least ten hours of individual therapy. I prayed about where I should go for more counseling and felt the Lord leading me to a female counselor who had been one of my professors. At this time, I was doing quite a bit of speaking across the country and had clients of my own. I entered therapy, sure I would have to spend only a month or two in it. Don and I were still having some sexual difficulties, so I determined this would be the area I would focus on. At the third session, Dr. Basbas sat down with me to go over some test results. Confidently I asked, "Well, how long do I have? A couple or three months?"

Dr. Basbas looked across the room at me and said, "Considering these test results, you could leave early at six months, or you could stay two years and really let God do the healing He wants to do in your life."

I'd love to tell you that I said, "Oh, thank you, wise counselor . . . , " but I didn't.

I looked her straight in the eye and said, "You don't understand. I'm famous. I've written a book on this subject." She calmly said, "Well, it's up to you."

I left that session angry. How dare she tell me I wasn't okay?! I went into a depression. I was ready to call the publisher with instructions to take all my books off the market. I thought, *If I'm not healed by now, I'll never be.*

Then the Spirit of God seemed to speak to my heart: *Jan, this does not mean I haven't healed you. It just means I want to do more. Are you willing?*

I said, "Yes, Lord."

I have shared this with victims all over. I spent two years in counseling, and it was the richest time I had spent so far. In the middle of that therapy I told the Lord I would be there five years if that's what He wanted. He touched areas I had totally avoided in therapy the first time. God is faithful in our lives to keep "removing the debris."

During this second therapy, we focused on the sexual difficulties I was having. As I shared some of the specifics, my therapist made a simple observation that the problems may not be due just to me. When she first said it, I didn't think she knew what she was talking about. Of *course,* the problems were my fault—I was the sexual abuse victim!

We did more investigating, though, and it soon became clear that part of Don's and my difficulty had to do with his pattern of emotional withdrawal. He explains this in detail in the "Walls" chapter. Essentially, what would occur was that Don would pull back from me emotionally due to some incident during the day. At night, having laid aside the issues of the day, he would come to bed primed for an intimate encounter. Then I would have trouble responding. We had always assumed this was my problem. After watching this pattern for nearly a month, I finally confronted Don.

FACING IT

I had said something to him early in the day that hit his emotional withdrawal button. He obviously had backed away from me. He was not unpleasant, but the emotional connection was not there. I sat down next to him and asked what had caused his withdrawal. We discussed the specifics, and then I simply said, "You know, we've had trouble connecting sexually in the last month, and I think a lot of it has to do with this pattern of emotional withdrawal."

We talked about how important it is for a woman to feel an emotional connection *prior to* entering into the sexual relationship. Men are wired differently. They often look to the sexual relationship *for* emotional expression. I expressed to Don that when he withdraws from me emotionally during the day, it is hard for me to feel amorous toward him at night. Don looked at me a little disgruntled.

"So what am I supposed to do about it?" he asked rather annoyed. "I suppose you want *me* to go to therapy!"

"Yeah, that might be a good idea," I said. "You know, honey, I've spent the last six years of our marriage working on my issues. I'm not saying that all the sexual problems are because of you. I'm just saying that I've been trying to work on mine and now it's only fair that you work on the areas you're responsible for."

Don sat there, silent.

I put my arms around him and said, "Don, I'm committed to you no matter what. If you decide not to get help, I won't divorce you. If you want this area of our relationship to improve, though, you have to do your part."

We ended that conversation and I never said another word about it. Three months later, Don started attending a church group for adult children of alcoholics. He has made a concerted effort to be aware of his emotional withdrawal pattern, and our sexual relationship has improved — it is better now than it has ever been.

Don and I have found that victims marry victims. If you are looking at your spouse as the one responsible for all the difficulties in your sexual relationship, look again — this time in the mirror. It takes two for a sexual relationship to work and it takes two when it is not working.

MALE AND FEMALE DIFFERENCES

It has become clear to us that the sexual relationship is complex. If it were not, there wouldn't be so many books written on the subject, even in the Christian realm. God made men and women different in this area. As Don and I have talked, we have seen how we are inverted in our responses to the physical, emotional and spiritual areas. Here is a diagram that may help to explain what I mean:

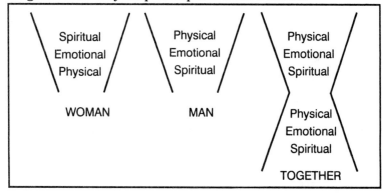

It seems Don is much more open and unrestricted in

the physical/sexual area whereas I am more open and un-restricted in the spiritual area. It's almost as though we enter into the other realms by coming through the broad-ened area first, but we are learning to complement each other and to develop more openness in the areas where we are naturally restricted.

When you consider the natural differences between a "normal" husband and wife, then compare a couple where each came from a dysfunctional home, you can see why problems mushroom. The Spirit quickened to my heart an analogy that we have shared on numerous occasions at our couples seminars that may help to illustrate.

Picture a man in a wheelchair. He has been confined to the chair all of his life. From the moment he rises in the morning until he is assisted to bed every evening, he re-mains in that chair. After all of these years, it has become a part of his identity. In fact, he feels lost without it, except for one time a week, the day he keeps his standing appoint-ment for physical therapy. The therapy consists of being in a warm, bubbling whirlpool for an hour. The man can hard-ly wait to get there each week. It's the only time he gets out of the confinement of that wheelchair. It's a time when he can feel a heightened sense of freedom and pleasure. He gets to "let loose" so to speak. He dreams about the whirlpool between appointments, and on the day of the appointment he wakes up with excitement and anticipation.

Now picture a little five-year-old girl. Her father is a harsh man with a military background. He has trained soldiers, and he runs his home the same way. He was an athlete in school and an excellent swimmer. He decides one day it's time for the five-year-old to learn to swim. He does not sign her up in a local swimming class, but decides to ex-pose her to the water himself. He marches her to the back-yard where the family whirlpool is. Without warning he throws her in.

She cannot swim, nor can she touch bottom. She

comes up for air only to hear her father say, "You're all right; just a few more minutes." Then he shoves her head back under the water. She feels she is going to die.

When she finally gets out of the whirlpool, she is terribly afraid of water. Her life now consists of constant fear that she may not survive her next "swimming lesson."

Now that you have firmly pictured in your mind the man in the wheelchair and the little girl, imagine that they marry each other. The whirlpool represents the sexual relationship. The man in the wheelchair is like Don and I am the little girl.

All his life, Don was confined to a world without feelings. He was restricted and restrained. He goes to the whirlpool with such eagerness that it resembles an obsession. The whirlpool is the only place he is able to feel really free. He can experience and express emotions there unlike any other place he has ever been.

I am the little girl who got thrown into adult sexual intimacy without warning. I was not prepared for the terror, the helplessness, the confusion. It is no wonder I fear the whirlpool and all it represents.

Don and I use this analogy to make clear to both partners what is happening. We light-heartedly share that in our relationship, the man in the wheelchair marries the little girl and says, "All right! Just what I've been waiting for! Let's you and me go to the whirlpool!"

"Oh, no!" the little girl shrieks in horror. "Not the whirlpool!"

We tell couples that the man in the wheelchair is not right with the little girl being wrong, nor is the little girl right and the man wrong. Rather, it is their different points of reference. We have had to learn this in our relationship. The man in the wheelchair has to be less obsessive in his need to go to the whirlpool, and he needs to develop other areas where he can get out of the confinement of his chair and experience freedom. The little girl has to begin to trust the man in the wheelchair not to force her head under water but to lovingly share the freedom of the whirlpool with her.

In practical terms, sometimes the man in the wheelchair comes ever so gently and asks the little girl to climb up on his lap so they can go sit by the whirlpool. He waits until the fear leaves her eyes, and then he says, "Do you think we can stick our feet in yet?"

"Yes, I think so, but don't get any funny ideas," warns the little girl.

Pretty soon, the warmth of the man's love and the tenderness of his touch calm the fears of the little girl. She immediately becomes a woman; they embrace, and they experience God's complete design for husband and wife.

REPAIRING THE PLUMBING

To the men, we would encourage you to do just as the man in the wheelchair has done. Learn to develop intimacy outside the bedroom. How is that done? By being willing to share your feelings with your wife. Sit down at the kitchen table and talk to her about things like where you want to be in your career in five years. Tell her about your childhood; hug her when she's cooking dinner—no strings attached—and pray with her, sharing your innermost desires; ask her what she cares about most deeply; be willing to spend an evening caressing and kissing—agree in advance that that's as far as it goes. As you invest in your relationship by sharing yourself, you will begin to see a response.

Be careful not to do these things with an ulterior motive; she will pick it up if you are insincere. You want to create emotional closeness with her. When she feels that closeness, she is better able to respond sexually.

A woman who has been sexually abused needs first of all to feel safe. She needs to know that she can trust you, that you love her for who she is, and that she has a choice with regard to sexual intimacy. If she feels she has no choice, watch out! Be careful of making demands in the name of "submission." Many men we have counseled have made this mistake, only to inflict more damage and cause more distance and hostility. Remember, Jesus laid His life down for us. In the same way, according to Ephesians 5:25, the husband is to lay his life down for his wife.

To the women, we encourage you to seek help if you have been a victim of sexual abuse. Some women who are going through the healing process need time to withdraw from sexual intimacy; however, you must recognize that men are physiologically different and may need your sensitivity as well. Work on recognizing some of the lies you believe about yourself, about men and about sex. Root those lies up with the help of the Holy Spirit, and ask God to replace in your heart the truth about what He intended the sexual relationship between a husband and a wife to be.

Most men who have come from dysfunctional backgrounds struggle with abandonment issues. Many of them fear that some day their wife will not need them anymore and she will be gone. They often react to those deep inner fears by becoming extremely controlling or very dependent. With your own healing, try to be clear on whose issue is whose, and put extra effort into creating an environment where your husband feels secure in your love. As you do this, he will be able to share more of himself with you.

ARE THE PROBLEMS EVER OVER?

As long as you are a homeowner, you probably will face plumbing problems.

In a marriage, inevitably there will be sexual problems. One of the most wonderful things Don ever said to me centered around a problem we were having in this area. Just last year some new memories were coming to the surface that previously had been repressed. Our sexual relationship had been fulfilling for quite some time, but it was particularly difficult for me to respond one evening.

Instead of being angry or asking me, "Why is this happening now after all this time?" Don simply drew me to him and held me tightly, and said, "Honey, it's okay. I plan to spend the rest of my life with you. If we're fortunate, we'll have forty or fifty more years together, and whether or not we make love tonight doesn't matter."

I knew the sincerity of Don's heart and it released me to love him even more.

In this chapter we've discussed some of the common sexual problems experienced by victims in marriage. We have underscored that it takes two to have a relationship work and both are involved when it is not working. We hope you will keep in mind the picture of the man in the wheelchair and the little girl. We pray that you will be encouraged and we assure you, this area does get better with time. Know that no matter what types of precautionary measures you take, some plumbing problems are inevitable. The following experience occurred one week after our bathroom sink incident described at the beginning of the chapter.

We had invited our special friends, Jerry and Jenny, over to watch the USC vs. UCLA football game with us and they brought along a delicious multi-layered dip. We all sat in our living room munching away while we watched the game. That dip was incredible! First, it had a layer of refried beans, then a layer of avocado; on top of that were tomatoes, then olives, cheese and sour cream. It was huge. When the game was over and Jenny, Jerry and their kids were gone, I went into the kitchen to clean up.

The dip was so large we had eaten only half of it. I knew it would not keep so I put it down the disposal. After letting the disposal run for a minute or so, I noticed a funny noise. I turned it off and opened the cupboard under the sink. The dip had been sprayed all over the inside of the cupboard! I began to gag.

Not quite sure what happened, I called to Don, and we looked at each other with that look that says, "Oh no, not again!"

Don then went into our bedroom to get something from his closet, and he stepped on a spot that squished beneath his feet.

"Jan," he called, "I think we have a real problem."

For a few minutes the scenario ran through our minds again. A main-line break? We investigated but found nothing else wet. I went to the kitchen to clean up the cupboard and discovered a hole in the disposal. Then I remembered what had happened in the bedroom.

"Honey," I called to Don, "it's okay. I just remembered. Before our company came, the water bottle I use for ironing fell over in front of your closet when I put the ironing board away."

Both of us dropped on the couch relieved. I reflected on this chapter and silently prayed, *Lord, please, no more real-life illustrations on plumbing for a while. I get the picture.*

All has been calm on the plumbing front since then. *Thank you, Lord!*

6

Repairing the Foundation

As I travel around the country, I am amazed at the different reactions I receive when someone asks me where I am from and I tell them I am a native Californian. Some people sigh with envy; others discount my credibility, while still others shake their heads and mumble something about earthquakes. I admit that living here all my life has not eased the queasiness I feel about earthquakes. Unlike other natural disasters, there is no forewarning and no time to prepare for the destruction that may be imminent.

A major earthquake centered about 25 miles from our home in October 1987. It hit the city of Whittier very hard. Many buildings were demolished. I will always remember when it hit. My two daughters and I were sitting at the dining table eating our breakfast when the rumble began. The oak hutch with my china and crystal in it started rattling. Heather and Kellie screamed and we ran to a doorway between our living room and den. Huddled there together, we prayed out loud. What started out as shaking turned into a series of minor jolts. It seemed to last forever, and I was alarmed. Finally, it stopped – but would another more serious one follow? I didn't know. Heather didn't want to go to school that morning and I didn't blame her. We sat together in the living room trying to get information from the television. It had centered close to our home and it was a big one—a 5.9 magnitude. I inspected the damage in our home and nothing was broken, but several pieces of my china had overturned and six crystal goblets lay pressed against the glass doors of my china cabinet.

DELAYED APPEARANCE OF DAMAGE

It wasn't until several months later that I discovered behind our living room drapes a long, thin crack starting at the ceiling and extending all the way to the floor. An interesting thing about earthquake damage is that it is not always immediately apparent. The news media usually goes to the scene of the rubble, and on TV we see the shattered windows, the huge cracks in the streets, and the destroyed businesses. What we don't see is the wreckage that is below the surface and that can appear even several years later.

Recently I asked our friend John, the building contractor, about the projects he was working on currently.

"We're working on a home in Whittier right now," he said. "Remember the earthquake that hit a couple of years ago?"

"How could I forget?" I replied.

"The house we're working on was damaged in that quake. The family has continued to live in it because it appeared to have suffered only minor damage, but about three months ago they noticed the doors were not closing properly. Then a window broke. Then the walls seemed to be rising. They thought they must be going crazy. Finally, they realized the floor was uneven, so they called in a structural engineer for an assessment. He discovered several fractures in the foundation."

"Do you mean they had been living there all that

time and the house could have collapsed underneath them? And they didn't know it?" I asked.

"That's right," John said.

I was instantly reminded of my childhood. Although I was molested between the ages of seven and ten, I had done a pretty good job of resuming my life. I knew those events had a dramatic effect on my life, but as an adult, I had convinced myself those issues had been resolved. I had "forgiven" my stepdad, so that was all there was to it.

DELAYED EVIDENCE OF EMOTIONAL DAMAGE

At twenty-five I had a promising career, a loving, Christian husband, a nice home, and a good relationship with the Lord. Two years into our marriage, our first daughter, Heather, was born. All of a sudden, my life was fractured. I was not suicidal, nor was I dysfunctional, at least not on the surface. I was like the house in Whittier. I had survived the destruction of the abuse in my childhood and had gone on living my life as normal. Bit by bit, though, my life began to show signs of the structural damage below the surface. I was mildly depressed. I would be fine for a few days, then hit a deep valley for several days. Anything could cast me into the valley of despair: a new recipe that failed; an innocuous comment made by Don; an oversight by someone at church; or a difficult day with my toddler.

I was angry. Enraged would be a more accurate word. Heather's crying seemed to set me off more than anything. I felt so out of control—I feared I could not control the rage inside. To my shame, I felt I had the potential of physically abusing my own child. I had a reservoir of criticism inside me and Don became my target. My nitpicking was driving a wedge between us. I was miserable.

Like the people in the house in Whittier, I could no longer ignore the obvious ruin. Yet what could I do? Where could I turn? I, too, had to call in a structural engineer. The Master Architect had to be consulted.

I confessed to the Lord that I was not happy with my life and I asked Him to change me.

Instead of instantly changing me by changing my outward symptoms, He seemed to say, *We've got to go back to the foundation.* He understood where the problem was.

If the family in Whittier had merely remedied the obvious surface problems, they would only have delayed inevitable devastation. More foundational work was required. I was intrigued by the similarity of the Whittier project as it related to my life. I had to find out more.

I asked John, "What happens now?"

"We have to tear it down and start from scratch," John replied.

"Wait a minute," I said. "Isn't there a way to repair it without having to destroy what is left?"

"In some cases that's true. Sometimes the damage to a foundation is not too extensive. In that case, you may be able to jack up the house and repair the damaged parts of the foundation. This time, however, there were so many fractures in different areas, and they went so deep, it was impossible to repair it and keep the house intact."

Suddenly, I felt the utter dismay this family must have felt when they were told the entire house had to be dismantled so the workers could get to the foundation. I knew what it was like to see everything you had worked for crumbling before your eyes.

DEBRIS REMOVAL

"What is the procedure, John?"

"After the house is removed, we start from scratch. We have to start over, just as if we were building there for the first time. The only difference is that we must take extra precautions to make sure all the organic material left in the soil has been removed."

"Organic material? What is that?"

"Anything that is subject to decay. We must remove whatever is in the soil that can corrupt its 'integrity.' For instance, we will re-scarify the topsoil—take off the top layer—but that is not enough. If we only removed the top-soil and neglected to remove the organic materials that lay deeply embedded, we would risk putting the foundation on something that might eventually decay," John explained. "There might be tree roots five feet underground. Even if you properly compacted the soil, eventually those roots would decay and could affect the foundation. Before we pour a new one, we want to make sure we get rid of all the debris."

I understood exactly what John was saying. God had initiated "debris removal" in my life eight years ago. I did not understand all He was trying to do then. In fact, I was frustrated that the Holy Spirit seemed to dig deeper and deeper into the pains of my past. *Why must I go through this, Lord? Isn't it enough that I experienced it? Do I have to go through the pain all over again? Won't you just let me go on and try to forget?* In response, the skillful hand of the loving Master Builder kept resolutely reaching into the recesses of my heart to remove all the debris.

"So let's say you've removed all the debris. How do you know what to do next?" I asked.

THE CRITICAL PATH METHOD OF REPAIR

"That's where the CPM comes into play," John replied with a smile.

"What's that?"

"It's the 'Critical Path Method.' Before they ever begin a project most builders sit down and devise their CPM. They put on paper the actual sequence of events for each job. They study the blueprints carefully to make sure that

Critical Path Method for Emotional Recovery

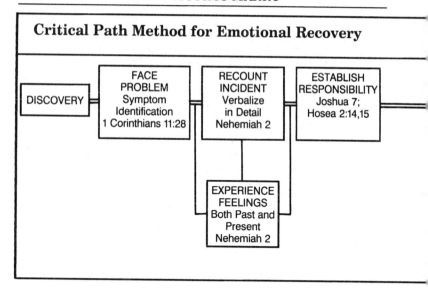

the sequence coincides with the overall building plan."

"I'm not sure what you mean," I stated, a bit confused.

"Let me give you an example. If the builder didn't plan the sequence of events in the building process carefully," John elaborated, "one of the subcontractors might come in and pour the slab before all the underground plumbing was completed. If that happens, the slab would have to be broken up and the plumbing work finished. The fewer mistakes, the more the builder saves. If he doesn't take the time to see that every segment of the process is carried out in order, he sets himself up to lose a lot of money and time."

"So, you mean the critical path method is like the directions on a recipe. It tells you in what order to add the ingredients."

"That's right," John said. "It is the detailed sequence of every phase of the project all the way to completion."

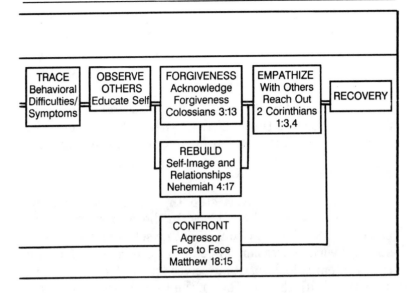

TEN STEPS TO RECOVERY

I realized then that God had designed a divine "critical path method" for me. Through recent years I have shared these steps with many individuals and in seminars, and the response has been overwhelming. Many who were not even victims of sexual abuse have written expressing appreciation for the steps. The steps provide direction, insight and resolution to issues of the present as well as the past.

The method is not magic, nor should it be undertaken frivolously. Nor is it a substitute for seeking wisdom from our Wonderful Counselor or for obtaining professional assistance when appropriate. Rather, it is a tool, a guide toward the resolution of hurts in our lives. In fact, it was through my own process of therapy that these ten steps emerged. They incorporate what we have discussed in this chapter so far. They prompt a discovery of the faulty foundation of our "house"; they initiate a removal of the debris; they prepare the soil; they make it possible to pour a new, dependable foundation.

The steps in this critical path method are illustrated on pages 106 and 107, and are briefly enumerated and explained below. They are further detailed in *A Door of Hope*, which I encourage you to read. (See the recommended reading list at the end of this book.)

Don and I advise couples to go through these steps together. Working through them with each other provides encouragement and momentum, and it enhances intimacy.

STEP 1: Face the Problem

This is the discovery step. In 1 Corinthians 11:28 we are told to "examine" ourselves. In the second year of my marriage, I had to look honestly at myself. I had to face my struggle with depression, anger and a critical spirit. Facing the problem is looking at ourselves truthfully. It is self-examination with the guidance of the Holy Spirit. I encourage individuals to pray Psalm 51:6 daily. It says: "Behold, You desire truth in the inward parts, and in the hidden part You will make me to know wisdom." As with the house in Whittier that began to show belated signs of earthquake damage in its windows, walls and floor, symptoms can seep out into our everyday lives, and we need to look at them and evaluate them. Here are some questions that may help you assess the need:

- Do you experience frequent periods of depression?
- Are you unreasonably angry with your spouse, children or boss?
- Do you have intense emotions that seem exaggerated in given circumstances?
- Do you feel intimidated, fearful, hostile or numb around members of your family?
- Do you feel ashamed or intensely guilty when you have failed or not met your own expectations?
- Have you always had difficulty getting close to others or allowing them to get close to you?

- Do you seem to have personality conflicts at work or with those in authority?
- Are you easily persuaded to do things you really don't want to do?
- Do you have difficulty identifying your feelings?
- Is it important that you maintain control over your situation?
- Do you feel panicked when things get out of control?
- Do you have little desire for sexual intimacy? Or are you sometimes obsessed by sexual desires?
- Do you feel unacceptable to God and to others?
- Do you find you cannot accept compliments without invalidating them?
- Are you relentless in your pursuit of perfection?

If you answered yes to some of these questions, ask the Lord to help you discover where the roots of these behaviors or emotions are. Discuss, explore and prayerfully consider these areas with your mate. Allow the Master Builder to illuminate any areas that may have been fractured, and pursue His plan toward restoration.

STEP 2: Recount the Incident

If a childhood memory came to your mind as you examined yourself, you may need to relate it. Retelling hurtful incidents does not change what has occurred, but does provide for an emotional release. Remember that the emotions of a child are real and should not be minimized.

The recounting step is similar to a grief process. The scriptural basis for this is Nehemiah 2. Nehemiah had a burden to rebuild the wall in Jerusalem. Prior to starting the building process he went out to survey the loss. The Scripture tells us he went from gate to gate, viewing and weeping over the destruction. It is necessary for us to survey the losses and damage in our lives before we set out to rebuild.

When you recount the incidents that the Holy Spirit

brings to your mind, try to detail them as much as you can. Do not discount as insignificant any incident God brings to your mind after prayer. Many times these "small" incidents are packed with fractured emotions that need expression (e.g., the loss of a childhood pet, an embarrassing experience in elementary school, the divorce of your parents).

It is important that this be done only with a person who will offer support and understanding. If you are married, and your spouse is not able to be that person, you may need to seek a professional or a knowledgeable lay person. I usually recommend the detailed recounting be done with persons of the same sex. The possible exceptions to this would be in the professional setting or within the marital relationship.

Recounting is the initial step of "removing the debris." For the total removal to be completed, there must be a connection of the emotions.

STEP 3: Experience the Feelings

This is the second step in removing the debris. If, as a result of the previous two steps, the Holy Spirit brought to your mind some event from childhood, or some recent event, it is important for you to focus on the feelings attached to that event. If you were never allowed to express or even experience emotions in childhood, this step may be difficult for you. It is important that you realize God made you an emotional being. He does not want our emotions to totally rule our lives, but He does want us to express them appropriately. It is important to know that **feelings do not age**. David Seamands, in *Healing of Memories,* states:

> Time by itself does not and cannot heal those memories which are so painful that the experiences are as alive and painful ten or twenty years later as they were ten or twenty minutes after they were pushed out of consciousness.[1]

When we continue to suppress intense feelings and

hold them in, they often work their way out into our behavior or into our body. The most common example is an ulcer. Medical studies substantiate that chronic stress and internalized anger show up in physical maladies.

Experiencing the feelings is part of the grieving process. For men who have difficulty in this area I recommend the book, *Healing the Masculine Soul,* by Gordon Dalbey.[2] Isaiah 53:4 (KJV) tells us that Jesus is the one who has "borne our griefs, and carried our sorrows," and in Hebrews 4:15 (KJV) we are told: "We have not an high priest which cannot be touched with the feeling of our infirmities; but was in all points tempted like as we are, yet without sin."

He understands all the feelings we have felt, past and present, and He desires that we bring the wounded part of ourselves to Him. Through the grieving process, we release emotions that have occupied valuable space in our hearts. This may take time, so don't rush the process. Remember God wants to do a complete debris removal so that the new foundation is established on solid ground.

STEP 4: Establish Responsibility

If God has brought to your heart a specific incident, you need to look at that event objectively in order to establish proper accountability. If you have a history of abuse, you are prone to react in one of two different ways: (1) You assume false responsibility and take on all the guilt for what has occurred; or (2) you push out all responsibility and project all blame onto others.

Most victims of abuse have carried their offenders' guilt for so long that it is difficult for them to assume proper responsibility in their everyday adult life. If you were abused as a child, you need to place the responsibility on the offender. This is a biblical step and actually paves the way toward forgiveness. We read several instances in Scripture where God established the accountability of people for their actions (e.g., David and Bathsheba, 2 Samuel 12; Achan,

Joshua 7).

Establishing responsibility does not mean we are justified in taking vengeance. That belongs to God. It does mean that we sort out where the accountability lies.

Many times, there are those who were not directly involved with the offense but who may be what I call co-contributors. My mother, who knew about the abuse but took no action to protect me, would be a co-contributor.

Remember, establishing responsibility is not the same as blaming. It is a balancing out of accountability before God. For further understanding I refer you to the chapter on establishing responsibility in *A Door of Hope.*

STEP 5: Trace Behavioral Difficulties/Symptoms

Robert Schuller once said we need to "face, trace and erase" the problems in our lives. This step of tracing behavioral difficulties and symptoms incorporates that concept and adds an additional phase: *Replace* dysfunctional patterns with healthy ones.

What does it mean to trace problem areas in our lives? It means we begin to look at *(face)* our current patterns, particularly those that involve our interpersonal relationships, and *identify* the undesirable characteristics that predominate. After we identify those behavioral patterns we wish to change, we *trace* them back to when and where they originated in our lives. After we, with the help of the Holy Spirit, have traced them back to the root, we set about by a disciplined approach to *erase* those unhealthy and damaging patterns. Finally, we seek God's wisdom and empowering to *replace* those destructive patterns by implementing more healthy ones. This is a pivotal step in the process. It is part of the "debris removal," and at the same time, it is a step in pouring the new foundation.

STEP 6: Observe Others/Educate Yourself

It is through this step we attempt to involve others in the process of our healing. The support group environment is extremely beneficial for victims of abuse. Right now we are seeing groups rise up all over our country, some of which are: ACA (adult children of alcoholics); overcomers groups for alcoholism, drug abuse and compulsive overeating; groups for terminal cancer patients and their families; Compassionate Friends, a group for bereaved parents. All of these groups provide something that is remarkably healing for someone who has experienced a particular struggle – and that is, someone else who has been through it. Being with others who have shared similar pain not only lets us know we are not alone, but it also provides insight and comfort during the tough times.

It may be necessary for you to seek outside help as you and your spouse examine patterns from your background. The objectivity of a specialized counselor or support group can speed the recovery process. It is crucial that you continue to educate yourself on your particular issues. Read books and articles, view documentaries, and tap the resources in your community. A recognized counselor in the area of repressed trauma, Dr. Arlyss Norcross, made a profound statement in a radio interview when she said, "You went through it (the pain) alone the first time; don't go through it alone again."

STEP 7: Confront the Aggressor

> **CAUTION**: DO NOT ATTEMPT CONFRONTATION
> ON THE BASIS OF READING THIS MATERIAL.
> THERE ARE OTHER PREREQUISITES THAT NEED
> TO TAKE PLACE BEFORE CONFRONTATION
> IS CONSIDERED OR ATTEMPTED.

In *A Door of Hope,* one entire chapter discusses confrontation. *Please* consult this chapter before proceeding with any type of confrontation.[3]

For our purposes here, let me say that confrontation is not always appropriate. If it is to occur, it should be surrounded by a great deal of prayer and seeking God's timing. Bringing these issues into the light should be done with the motive of reconciliation. Confrontation is a way to put responsibility in the hands of the rightful owners. Many people attempt it prematurely, hoping it will bring quick resolution. This usually does not happen. Rich Buhler, noted Christian talk-radio host and author, says, "Confrontation needs to come from our healing, not from our hurt."

When confrontation is indicated, it is helpful to consult an objective third party and to practice the confrontation prior to a face-to-face meeting with the offender. This often provides important feedback that can prevent a premature confrontation, or it can help you prepare for possible responses from the offender. The primary objective should be truth balanced by love. In 1 John 1:7 we read:

> If we walk in the light as He is in the light, we have
> fellowship with one another, and the blood of Jesus
> Christ His Son cleanses us from all sin.

Confrontation is an opportunity for all to walk in the light, and as a result, to experience fellowship and the cleansing that is possible only through the complete work of Christ on the cross.

STEP 8: Acknowledge Forgiveness

This step is often most emphasized by Christians. Forgiveness is a vital part of the healing process, but it is not the only part. I have counseled many Christians who have entered into what I call "quick" forgiveness. In an attempt to be obedient to Scripture they have given mental assent to forgiveness without letting their heart be healed. If forgiveness is to have its full effect upon us and toward others, it must transcend the intellect and encompass the emotions as well.

Before we can truly extend forgiveness to another person, we must first acknowledge that an injury has occurred and that we have experienced pain from that injury. It is in recognizing that pain and working through it that forgiveness becomes a priceless gift offered to the one who has hurt us. By acknowledging forgiveness we are not condoning the actions of the offender. We are, however, acknowledging the complete work of Christ's blood on the cross, for, in light of the cross, there is no difference between the offender and the offended. We all are in need of His shed blood "to cleanse us from all unrighteousness" (1 John 1:9*b*).

STEP 9: Rebuild Self-Image and Relationships

This step is imperative to growth. In Romans 8:29 we are told we are "being conformed to the image of His Son." When we have grown up with a faulty foundation or have experienced painful events that have scarred us emotionally, we need to be rebuilt.

Many of the self-help books out today talk about improving your self-esteem through various activities, accomplishments or accolades. I am utterly convinced that the process of improving your self-esteem must fully rest on internalizing the Word of God. In *A Door of Hope* I discuss the process of recognizing the lies we have believed about ourselves and about God, rooting out those lies with the help of the Holy Spirit, and replacing them by introducing the truth of God's Word into the heart. As I have done this in my life, the change has been incredible. It has carried the truth of God's Word from my head to deep within my heart.

Because of the hurtful experiences I went through, my image of God was distorted. I asked God to show me His Father's heart of love for me. He has been faithful, as I have sought Him for wisdom, to restore my relationships to wholeness. Learning to integrate the Word of God and allow the Holy Spirit to touch and heal the broken places in my life has been the solidarity of my recovery. God's Word has been the "re-bar" that makes the foundation firm.

STEP 10: Express Concern/Empathize With Others

Expressing concern and empathizing with others provides hope. As I share my personal experience all over the country, I am continually in awe of the grace of God. He allows us to comfort others with the comfort we have received from Him (see 2 Corinthians 1:4), and it is a blessing in our lives. It is important in this step that we have our priorities in order.

Oswald Chambers said, "It is the work that God does through us that counts, not what we do for Him."[4] He is able to redeem any situation in our lives if we are willing to place it all in His hands. As we proclaim that message to others, He is honored, and Isaiah 58:12 comes to pass:

> Those from among you
> Shall build the old waste places;
> You shall raise up the foundations of many
>   generations;
> And you shall be called the Repairer of the Breach,
> The Restorer of Streets to Dwell In.

If by reading this book thus far you realize you have a fractured foundation, take heart. The steps we have outlined were designed to help you, from discovery all the way through to recovery, under the guidance of the Holy Spirit. If you are willing to implement this "critical path method" as appropriate to your individual situation, God will complete His work. If you will commit yourself to permitting God's Spirit to "remove the debris," He will not only repair the structural damage, He will pour a new foundation in your heart. We are told in 1 Corinthians 3:11: "No other foundation can anyone lay than that which is laid, which is Jesus Christ." He is willing; are you?

"Faithful is He that calleth you, who also will do it"
(1 Thessalonians 5:24, KJV).

7

Framing the House

Ron and Karen Jensen have been friends of mine for more than ten years. I met Ron while I was still a waitress working my way through college. He and Karen married in 1978 and lived not far from me. They were a tremendous support during my single years, allowing me to converge upon them on those weekend nights when being alone at home became almost unbearable. They always had an open ear to listen, and were a mainstay that last year of courtship with Don. Karen was a bridesmaid in our wedding and even made our beautiful three-tiered wedding cake.

Not long ago they purchased another home in Orange County, California, near where they were living. Don, the girls and I recently went to see them and we all took a trip over to their future home, which was still under construction. They shared with us all the details of having obtained their home, including how they were on a huge waiting list for these homes, and how fortunate they were to get one.

Here in Southern California, builders often build tracts in phases, limiting the number of homes in each phase, and offering some minor variations from phase to phase. The main differences are the completion dates, the floor plans and square footage, and the cost. Ron and

Karen's house was almost finished. We toured the lovely new home, which included a spacious kitchen, a huge master bedroom with a fireplace, and an exquisite oak bannister, which curved along the stairway. After the tour, Ron took us to see some of the other homes in the tract. Each of the four groups was at a different stage, or phase, of construction.

We went first to Phase IV, the last group that would be completed, where the builders were just beginning the underground plumbing and electrical work. They had not leveled any of the lots, nor had any of the foundations been poured.

Next we went to the Phase III group. There the foundations had been poured and you could see the cement slabs with plumbing pipes protruding from the ground, along with the steel reinforcing bars that secure the foundation. In a couple of the houses in this phase, the builders were just beginning to do some of the wood framing.

Then we advanced to the Phase II homes. These houses were beginning to take shape. The framing allowed us to see the internal structure of the home and begin to distinguish between the rooms. The framed house looks like a maze. The wooden boards, perfectly aligned, nailed to other perpendicular boards, provide form and support.

I was surprised that here in California, the wood framing in the interior of the house is merely covered with drywall. Rarely are interior walls insulated. Even exterior walls of the house have only a slight amount—just batt insulation, tarpaper secured by chicken wire, and then covered over by the stucco.

I had pictured a flat piece of plywood on each side of the wood frame, encasing the entire home, interior walls included. I should have known this was not the case, just by experience. How many times had I tried to put up towel racks, only for them to pull out of the wall because the dry wall could not support the weight and because I had not found the "stud"?

"It seems odd," I said, "that there is no more to the interior walls than the framing and the drywall."

Our friend Ron continued to drive along, then pointed to a house and said, "You see that one? They put plywood on outside walls to provide more stability and added fire protection. That house has the plywood sheet on the exterior wall that leads into the garage. You have to remember, Jan, they want to put as little material into it as they can get by with, because it costs them less. Plus, here in California, we don't need as much insulation as they do in the colder climates."

As we drove along that day, we saw almost every stage of the construction process. I thought about the framing of a house, and I realized that it does several important things: It provides internal structure and uniqueness; it also provides appropriate boundaries inside the home.

INTERNAL STRUCTURE AND UNIQUENESS

Just as there needs to be form and structure in the construction of a home, there needs to be form and structure in a relationship. God has provided that form and structure in His Word. He tells us clearly in Ephesians 5:21-33 what the form is to be. He has outlined instructions to wives, to husbands and to both. Most of us have heard these instructions over and over, if we've spent any time in church, Sunday school or listening to radio or television preachers — but have we really heard?

What are the basic instructions to wives? Submit and respect. I know some of you women are reading this and saying, "If I hear that one more time, I'm going to be sick!" Most of the time, men instruct women about what they should be doing, and women instruct men about what they should be doing — and we face a standoff. The key is for each spouse to focus on what God has said, regardless of what the mate is doing.

I realized a couple of years ago that I really did not respect Don. It is difficult to submit to someone you don't trust or respect. I knew that I was commanded to, but did not find the substance of respect in my heart. I began to pray about it. I told the Lord I knew I was not following His direction and asked Him to expose the rebellion in my own heart and to make clear what was contributing to my lack of respect for Don.

Shortly after this, I asked Don if he would attend a counseling session with me. My therapist and I had discussed the advantages of having Don come in and take part in the therapy process. I had been in therapy for about ten months.

Don came in with me and spent a few minutes with Dr. Basbas before she called me in. After discussing some issues, Dr. Basbas turned to Don and asked him to share with me what he had told her before I came in. Don proceeded to tell me that he felt very unsupported by me, and continued with, "Remember about a week ago, when I was on that walk to Jerry's? I told you before I left that I wanted to go the seven or eight miles to his house, and then have you pick me up there."

"I remember," I said, unaware that Don was upset over anything. "You left around 4 P.M. and I got dinner all ready. You told me to leave the house at 6:15 to come and get you, and I did."

"Well," Don said, "do you remember that when you reached me, I was about a mile short of reaching Jerry's house? You stopped the car and asked me if I wanted to finish or if I just wanted to get in the car and go home so we could go eat dinner. I knew you didn't really want me to finish, so I just got into the car and we went home. I was really mad at you for that. You didn't even encourage or support me to go on and finish."

"What did you want me to say?" I asked.

"You could have said, 'Oh, honey, you're almost there; go ahead and finish your walk,' " Don said.

I was getting a little upset by this point. I asked, "If that walk was so important to you, why didn't you just say, 'Jan, it's important to me that I finish. I'll meet you at Jerry's in twenty minutes'?"

Don replied, "I knew, by the tone of your voice, you just wanted me to get into the car and go home. So I did."

By this time, I was ticked. "I don't respect that. If you don't have enough guts to do what you want, then don't hold me accountable when you choose to acquiesce to my wishes."

MUTUAL SUBMISSION

We definitely did not see eye to eye on this one! Later, when a couple of months had passed, I was able to admit to Don that I really had not wanted him to finish the walk because of the inconvenience to me, but that I couldn't respect him as a man or as head of the house if he gave in to what he thought I wanted. Don reminded me that I can be quite stubborn and persuasive at times, and that sometimes it's easier not to "buck the system." We were able to talk about this and I agreed to pray about the selfishness in me that wants to assert my will, if he would work on standing up for what he wants to do.

I continued to ask God to change my heart and teach me to walk in submission to my husband, and the Lord has shown me that He designed the relationship between a husband and a wife to be one of mutual submission. I am to submit to and respect Don as I would the Lord, regardless of Don's response. Don is to love me and lay down his life for me, as Christ did for the church, regardless of my response. We have found that when we do our parts as individuals there is no room for fear, domination or ruling over each other, or for either of us taking the other for granted.

I do not advocate a woman staying in an abusive

relationship. I do not think God ever calls a woman to suffer in silence that she might "win" her husband to the Lord. I think Chuck Swindoll put it well when he wrote:

> It is unrealistic and unfair to think that regardless of sure danger and possible loss of life, a godly mate and helpless children should subject themselves to brutality and other forms of extreme mistreatment. At that point, commitment to Christ supersedes all other principles in a home. I am not advocating divorce . . . but I do suggest restraint and safety via a separation. . . .

> It is one thing to be in subjection. It is another thing entirely to become the brunt of indignity, physical assault, and sexual perversion, and uncontrolled rage. Since the believer's body is the temple of God's Spirit, it is unthinkable that He is pleased to have our bodies mauled and mistreated by sick and/or thoughtless mates who care little about their family's welfare and think of nothing but their own twisted gratification.[1]

A CHANGE OF HEART

As I got serious with God about doing my part, He began to change my heart. About a year after we had our discussion on respect, another issue came up. We received an invitation to a wedding of one of Don's friends whom I'll call Craig. This was Craig's third marriage.

To be honest, I was not thrilled about going to this wedding or about buying another wedding gift for this guy. From my viewpoint, he was a flake who married younger women due to his own immaturity. I kept complaining as the wedding approached, harping on the fact that we had to buy the guy and "the new wife" a wedding gift.

Finally, Don had had it. I was in our bathroom rehearsing my objections when Don came to the door and said firmly but calmly, "Look, Jan, Craig is my friend, and I'm going to his wedding. If you don't want to get the gift,

I'll do it. If you don't want to go, it's up to you, but I'm going."

Basically, I interpreted that as, "Woman, you are out of line!"

I did not immediately change my attitude about going to the wedding, but later that day, I went to Don and thanked him. He had stood up in a way that made me respect him, and made me realize what a bad attitude I had. I bought the present later that week and we attended the wedding — together.

The internal structure of the home is erected on the basis of the floor plan. Of course, not every house is built with the same floor plan. So it is in marriage. In some relationships more "space" is needed than in others. God gives us guidelines that will insure a sound structure, but He does not dictate every aspect of the relationship. He takes into account our individuality and uniqueness. I know many couples who divide the household chores, paying the bills, and caring for the children. We have a great deal of freedom to differentiate the internal workings of our family as long as we stay within God's framework. As you look at the internal structure of your relationship, you may find areas that do not quite line up with God's design. Be willing to focus individually on your own part and give God room to change YOU!

Next, we're going to look at the stages of framing the relationship, putting up walls and setting up boundaries.

8

Walls of Support
Walls of Division

In the last chapter we talked about our friends, Ron and Karen, whose house we toured. As we walked through their home, Ron pointed out different defects he had observed that would need correction. One obvious one was in the living room by the fireplace.

The fireplace had a lovely mantle supported by two pillar-like columns, one on each side. We noticed some pencil marks on the drywall, near the gas valve—an arching arrow that indicated the valve was to be moved. As we looked closer, we saw that the fireplace gas valve had not been lined up properly. The right pillar of the fireplace totally covered the valve, preventing access. The builders had taken off the pillar so the valve could be moved, and in order to do this, the drywall would have to be punched through, the gas line extended, the drywall replaced, and the pillar joined again to the mantle. It was clear to me that the building process takes a great deal of forethought if repairs down the line are to be avoided.

The next stage in the construction is insulation and stucco on all exterior walls; then come the windows, and finally the interior drywall.

Just as in framing the house, a certain amount of forethought is necessary in framing the relationship when victims marry. Since some of our structure was already in place before we began to examine our faulty foundations, Don and I have had to make the repairs as they come to our attention. One of these areas has been the walls in our relationship. In the construction of a house, there are basically two types of walls: a partition wall that is merely a separating wall to distinguish between rooms, and a "bearing" wall which looks like any other wall in the structure but is constructed to bear the weight of the roof, etc. Bearing walls carry the weight directly to the foundation, which has been designed to take it. Let's look at the walls in our relationships, walls of support and walls of partition, or division.

PARTITION WALLS FOR PRIVACY

Can you imagine what it would be like to live in a place without any interior walls? I know it has been done and still is being done in some cultures, but it is not my idea of a healthy environment. Partition walls provide for a healthy separation of space. This creates an environment of protection, peace and privacy, all important ingredients in a healthy home.

One sure sign of a dysfunctional home is when no privacy or "boundaries" exist. In a home without boundaries, no one has the right to exist separately from other members of the family. Sometimes this is referred to as an "enmeshed" family.

In my growing-up home there was no such thing as guaranteed privacy. We were not allowed to lock the bathroom door and rarely could have our doors closed without permission. Even when I was a teenager, my stepdad would walk in on me while I was dressing, bathing or using the bathroom. The lack of modesty and privacy in our home was labeled "openness." As a result, there was no space in which I felt protected in my own home. The violation of proper boundaries often leaves a person with feelings of fear and exposure, and it robs them of personal dignity.

Don and I have attempted to be sensitive to our girls in this area. I have allowed Heather and Kellie to begin to set their own boundaries as appropriate. It is perfectly healthy to have times when one retreats from the other members of the family. In fact, when you have children, it is necessary for your sanity that time be set aside for you to be alone.

This summer we had the wonderful opportunity to take our daughters to Hawaii on vacation. Everyone was excited. Don and I had been there a few years ago by ourselves and knew that the girls would be thrilled by the tropical paradise. We spent weeks preparing. Don loves planning trips, and he involved the girls in his planning this time, using the occasion as an educational adventure. Prior to leaving, both Heather, eight, and Kellie, five, could recite the names of all the Hawaiian islands, knew the difference between the windward and leeward sides (which is still a mystery to me), had memorized common Hawaiian words and phrases, and were singing Hawaiian melodies. Finally, our departure date arrived, and soon we were in "paradise." The first three days were packed with activities. We were up early in the morning, off to breakfast, sightseeing, swimming, the beach, lunch, more swimming, sightseeing, dinner, shopping and to bed. At night, after getting the girls ready for bed, there was no time, nor space, for private conversation. When you're in a hotel room with kids, you feel obligated to retire early so they can sleep.

By the end of the third evening I was drained. Here we were in "paradise" and the routine of life had followed me. I was still saying things like, "Heather, go brush your teeth. Kellie, quit bugging your sister. Girls, hurry up and get dressed. Don't be running around. Stop that!" Don and

I were not communicating.

I woke up the fourth day and could take it no longer. I told Don I must have some quiet time. They went off to breakfast while I stayed in the room to have some prayer time. Through that short time, I realized I had not been communing with God and my relationships with the others showed it. The harmony, or lack of it, that I have in my relationships with my husband and children is in direct proportion to the time I spend with the Lord. How often I neglect my relationship with God and try to make human relationships work by my self-effort.

It is important in every relationship that some partition walls be erected to provide protection, peace and privacy. Later in the chapter Don will discuss unhealthy partition walls. We have struggled with some that have become dividers in our relationship. Just now, let's look for a moment at the "bearing" walls.

BEARING WALLS

As we mentioned earlier, bearing walls are constructed to bear the weight of the house and take that weight to the foundation. A house cannot stand without at least four bearing walls. Don and I discussed this concept, and I asked him what he thought one of the bearing walls was in our relationship.

He said simply but profoundly, "Like-mindedness. We're going in the same direction."

We are not the same two people, but we are one flesh, working together, setting goals and aspirations that are not at odds with each other. I thought of a song that Stormie Omartian sang a few years ago with the words: "I'm believing for the best in you . . . " That is really what marriage is all about, a willingness to believe in the best of and for your mate and yourself.

The like-mindedness Don spoke about centers

around our individual commitment to each other and to the Lord—a bearing wall in our relationship.

Jesus tells us in Matthew 11:28-30:

> Come to Me, all you who labor and are heavy laden, and I will give you rest. Take My yoke upon you and learn from Me, for I am gentle and lowly in heart, and you will find rest for your souls. For My yoke is easy and My burden is light.

In all relationships there will be times when it seems you cannot carry the weight anymore. Take heart. Jesus is our burden-bearer. God promised in Isaiah 28:16: "Behold, I lay in Zion a stone for a foundation, a tried stone, a precious cornerstone, a sure foundation." Jesus is that foundation and He calls you to come!

HEALTHY WALLS – Don

More than twenty years ago there was a movement in education to allow more freedom for children. It was called the "open classroom" concept. Educational leaders thought that by taking down walls in schools young people would be more spontaneous and curious and they would learn more efficiently. Round-shaped schools without walls were popular. However, one of the first things classroom teachers did was to erect their own walls within the open area. In addition, students felt threatened in the open environment; they had a difficult time focusing on the tasks at hand.

Large sums of money were then spent in constructing new walls or in totally remodeling buildings to bring schools back to the original classroom concept. The open classroom had failed. Partition walls were necessary to insure a quality, healthy educational environment.

As Jan described above, building a home is no different. Walls within the main frame of the house are a necessary and healthy part of home construction. They provide places of privacy within the home itself, places where family members can withdraw in a positive sense and be alone for purposes of study, reflection and personal hygiene.

Our friend, Pat, realizes this basic need. In his house he knocked out a wall to expand a closet, in which he placed a desk, a chair and a sound system. He sound-proofed the walls and uses this converted closet as a private place of refuge where he can read, work, or listen to his favorite music. This is good for Pat, as long as he spends only a healthy amount of time there and does not make a habit of withdrawing from his wife Brenda and their two sons. Pat's family knows of his special quiet place, and they respect it.

WALLS OF DIVISION

However, we also can create partition walls that are divisive and damaging to the marriage relationship. These walls are built by withdrawing emotionally from our mate. Emotional distancing, as it is sometimes called, is a withdrawal that disconnects us from another person. When we emotionally distance ourselves from our mate, it is like barricading ourselves in a room. Once barricaded, it is difficult to get out, even though we may really want to.

Emotional distancing has been a problem area in our relationship. During the first basketball season after we married, I had concocted a special strategy to defeat the league's favored team. I thought that by employing my "brilliant" strategy we had a chance to win. It turned out that we were overwhelmed by an obviously superior team, and my game plan failed miserably. When Jan picked me up after the game, she innocently and correctly commented that the strategy hadn't worked very well. I took the comment as a personal rejection and clammed up for days. I got myself as far away emotionally as I could. I would show HER not to criticize me anymore! I tried to punish her for being honest. I built a wall and barricaded myself from her.

EMOTIONAL DISTANCING

In most cases, it is the man who withdraws and distances himself from his wife. In *The Dance of Anger*, Dr. Harriet Lerner states that in each relationship there is an emotional pursuer and an emotional distancer.

> It is most often the woman who is the emotional pursuer and the man who is the emotional distancer. When the waters are calm the pursuer and distancer seem like the perfect complementary couple. When the waters are rough, however, each exaggerates his or her own style, and that's where the trouble begins.[1]

The pursuing woman who longs for emotional closeness and the logical, unresponsive distancer will have problems in many areas. If you must add to this the fact that the woman has been sexually traumatized, as in our relationship, you introduce a whole new set of predictable patterns that cause problems in a relationship.

When a husband begins to educate himself on the dynamics of abuse, he often gains a new understanding and empathy for his wife and her behavior. By gaining new insight, men often believe that their sexual relationship with their wife will automatically improve. They erroneously think that all the problems in relating sexually belong to the wife. I know. I was one of those men. Finally, I had to take stock of unhealthy patterns in my own life that were contributing to our sexual disharmony. We recently received this letter, which describes some common issues in this area:

Dear Jan,

I'll get right to the point. If I'm not perfectly happy and sexy and efficient at all times, my husband — a spirit-filled Christian — totally withdraws from me.

I'll use last night as an example. By the time he finally got home at 7 P.M. I'd had a rough time with our three young children, so I was far from being the "happy little homemaker." Basically, I was depressed, something he has very little understanding for. When I didn't respond in a perfectly loving way, he said, "Don't you like me at all?"

This attitude has been our number one handicap. He takes my problems personally, rather than seeing them as things we both need to work through. Last night, instead of asking what the real problem was, which had nothing to do with him, he immediately felt hurt and rejected.

During the first half of our marriage, I struggled with low self-esteem and the adjustment of a regular sex life because I had been sexually abused for nearly ten years by my father. My husband took these problems all along as a personal attack against him as a man and husband . . . We get along great when I'm acting perfect and fulfilling his sexual needs . . . He says that is what keeps us close, and yet when I have a bad day or fail him in any way he won't speak to me all evening.

I just don't know how much longer I can carry this burden . . .

This letter could have been written by Jan early in our marriage. I, too, was quite content to see Jan's lack of sexual desire as an attack on my masculinity or as her problem. I would withdraw and emotionally distance myself from her to protect myself from the pain of rejection. We spent an awful lot of time playing this game and neither of us saw the destructive patterns we were establishing. I had to learn some important things about facing my own issues and about understanding my wife.

Sexual closeness does not necessarily mean emotional closeness to a woman. Jan has told me that she must feel emotionally connected to me *before* she can enter into the intimacy of the sexual arena. As a man, I tend to pursue the area of physical sexual satisfaction in an effort to feel emotionally close. When this distancing has become a pattern of either mate, it takes its toll on the sexual relationship. Emotional distancing may occur as a *result* of existing disharmony in the sexual area, which only exacerbates the problem. Both partners need to examine ways in which they contribute to the problem, and they each need to take appropriate action.

The Penners, in their book *The Gift of Sex,* indicate that "women tend to shut down when they are unfulfilled sexually and men tend to feel more sexual hunger with lack of fulfillment."[2] Now relate this concept to a woman who has been sexually victimized. She often avoids sexual intimacy because of her past. The husband, who is not being fulfilled in this area, pursues even more. The woman withdraws more, feeling threatened by her husband's intensity. The man feels rejected and emotionally withdraws which, in turn, leaves the woman feeling disconnected and unable to respond to her husband. Does this sound like a never-ending cycle? It can be unless both partners take personal responsibility for their own issues.

You may be asking, "How do we overcome this complex predicament?"

TEARING DOWN THE WALLS OF DIVISION

Since emotional distancing is a major contributing factor, let's look at some concrete ways a couple can tear down these walls of emotional division.

Step 1: Recognize

As in any problem, recognition is the first step in beginning to correct it. Either the husband or the wife must begin to recognize when emotional distancing is taking place. You can recognize you are in an emotionally distant state when your natural inclination is to withdraw and not communicate with your mate.

Step 2: Communicate

Jan and I have made an agreement to go to each other when either of us feels distancing taking place. It will feel awkward at first, but it is the next step in breaking down that wall. Being able to express the fact that I am feeling distant has helped us interrupt the cycle and has resulted in less remoteness in our relationship.

Merely telling your mate what you are feeling is not a guarantee that the distancing will not continue. Sometimes you will be unable to bridge the gap. Sometimes emotional distancing has nothing to do with your mate and he or she needs to know this. It's possible that the everyday busyness of life, with all of its distractions, can be the culprit. It may help to provide some guidelines for communicating this information.

DO own your feelings by saying something like: "I'm not sure why this is happening, but I'm feeling distant from you right now."

DON'T blame your mate by saying anything like: "Ever since you got back from (shopping, golfing, etc.), you have been in your own world. You have withdrawn from me again."

DO let your mate know when you know the source: "Honey, I'm feeling distant right now from everyone. An incident with a kid at school has really upset me. I need some time to work this out."

We have found that sometimes physical distance can lead to emotional detachment. This is true especially for Jan when I am away for any length of time. As a basketball coach, I have attended our National Coaches Convention in the spring for the last twelve years. It is the national tournament, better known as the "final four," in which the final four collegiate teams in the nation compete for the Division I title. It is a great time for me to see some of my old coaching friends while at the same time I'm surrounded by basketball hysteria for the five days of the convention.

Something strange seems to happen to Jan while I am gone, though. Although she misses me, you'd never know it when I return home. She clicks into her "self-sufficiency" mode and is unable to reconnect with me right away. As we have discussed this, Jan has shared that she feels abandoned, much like she did as a child.

Although she understands this, it takes her a while to warm up to me again. She seems to put a wall around herself that says, "I don't need you; I can take care of myself." It usually takes a day or so for her to adjust to me being back home. Since we are both aware of this, and have spent time talking about it, the distancing has decreased and the closeness of our relationship returns more quickly.

Step 3: Determine the source

If you are experiencing emotional distancing from your mate, try to determine the source of your feeling. Talk about the feeling with your mate and try to think about other times in your life when you had similar feelings. Pray and ask God to show you where that feeling originated. Often when we are experiencing intense feelings, the present circumstance is just the catalyst of former unresolved feelings. Once you have determined the source, ask the Holy Spirit to heal those hurts. Be open to the possibility that you may need some outside assistance in this process.

A final word to you men. Don't be afraid to share your feelings. This is the best way to break down those walls that are isolating you from the woman you love. By sharing what is on your heart, the walls of your own defenses begin to crumble. As you choose to be vulnerable, the emotional distancing will begin to disappear. Psalm 18:29 is a promise we all can claim: "For by You I can run against a troop, and by my God I can leap over a wall."

OTHER WALLS – Jan

In addition to walls of support and walls of division, for our own protection, we sometimes create other walls that can destroy a solid relationship. One of these walls became obvious to me two summers ago when Don, the girls and I vacationed in Lake Tahoe. Certain details of our trip did not go just right. I had not anticipated Don playing golf an extra day, the condo did not meet our expectations, and we were struggling through some issues as a couple. Toward the end of the trip, I became more and more distant.

As I looked at that distance later, I realized it was due to feelings of abandonment. The more I felt Don left me to handle everything myself, the angrier I became. I was also feeling very lonely and isolated from him. While we were driving home, I sat silently in the car, hands clenched tightly together. We had not spoken a word for more than an hour. The pain in my heart was deep. Finally, I began to pray. "Lord, I hate it when it is like this. Can't Don see that I am hurting? Why does he just sit there?"

Very clearly, the Spirit of God spoke to my heart and said, *Jan, when are you going to stop taking refuge behind the wall of anger?* The question pierced me like a knife. The Spirit continued, *Knowing where Don came from, how can you expect him to reach through that enormous wall of anger? There is no way he is able to do that, and until you stop hiding behind that wall, no change will occur.*

I was pricked to the heart and tears began to roll down my cheeks.

About that time, Don looked over at me and saw the tears. Without a word, he reached out and squeezed my hand. Immediately that wall began to collapse. It was as if the Spirit was showing me that, if I would be willing to be vulnerable with Don rather than run behind a wall, he'd respond. That was a turning point in our relationship.

During my private devotions one day, almost a year

later, I came across a verse in Ezekiel 13:14 that actually describes the process I have gone through in breaking down the walls of division. It says:

> So I will break down the wall you have plastered
> with untempered mortar, and bring it down to the
> ground, so that its foundation will be uncovered; it
> will fall, and you shall be consumed in the midst of it.
> Then you shall know that I am the LORD.

Through this verse, the Lord showed me that I had erected walls of protection with my own self-effort (untempered mortar), and those walls must come down. Notice that He says He will uncover the foundation. He will show us where it originates—where the wall was set up. The wall will fall, and we will feel overwhelmed or "consumed." God allows us to go through some of this that we might learn to find our refuge in Him rather than in any other place. The verse clearly states that the end result is that we will know the Lord. As I have walked through this process, it has not been without pain, but I have discovered the futility of raising walls to insure my own protection. I am learning to run to Him with the words of David in Psalm 61:1-4:

> Hear my cry, O God; Attend to my prayer. From the
> end of the earth I will cry to You, when my heart is
> overwhelmed; lead me to the rock that is higher than
> I. For You have been a shelter for me, and a strong
> tower from the enemy. I will abide in Your taber-
> nacle forever; I will trust in the shelter of Your wings.

I know God understands. He knows my past and how difficult it has been to learn to surrender and trust Him. He has asked me to stop building—and taking refuge in—my homemade walls of self-protection. He knows these walls only rob me of what my heart is really hungry for.

He may be asking you to do the same thing. Will you choose today, to lay down your bricks and mortar and run to His sheltering wings?

He is waiting. Trust Him.

9

*Insulation
Vs. Isolation*

We have discussed the framing of the house that provides internal structure and uniqueness and have examined walls of support and walls of division. Let's now look at proper protection of the home (insulation) versus improper, or unhealthy, protection (isolation).

INSULATING YOUR HOME

When we moved into our home five years ago we became aware of a rebate program initiated by the gas company in our area. They were offering rebates to anyone who took measures toward making their homes more energy efficient through insulating the attic and the water heater, caulking and/or weather-stripping the windows, installing lower flow shower heads and duct wrapping, and insulating walls, floors and pipes. To qualify for the rebate, the homeowner needed to have a minimum of three of the above items. The gas company sent a representative to the home to verify the work and the rebate was determined according to the specific areas insulated. We received $322.00 from that rebate which essentially paid for our attic insulation.

Besides that, we have noticed a significant difference since insulating the attic. Our home remains decidedly cooler in the summer and warmer in the winter.

To insulate, according to Webster's dictionary, is to "place in a detached situation to prevent transfer of electricity, heat or sound; to prevent an undesired flow." It is a form of protection that keeps undesirable "influences" out.

In California, insulation is required only on the exterior walls of the building and under the roof. That's enough to provide protection from the weather conditions, and it also gives satisfactory soundproofing.

INSULATING YOUR MARRIAGE

In a marriage there are certain ways in which we can insulate our relationship, including prayer, communication, intimacy and a sensitivity to outside influences. One of the most important reasons for our writing this book has been that our hearts have been grieved over the number of Christian marriages we have seen crumble before our eyes. Many times this breakdown was due to denial about their faulty foundations. Couples or individuals who refuse to examine their past inadvertently re-enact destructive patterns that fracture relationships.

As victims of a dysfunctional family, we must be especially aware of our vulnerabilities. People who grow up not having their needs met are often on the lookout. They are, oftentimes, emotionally starving. If these needs are not recognized and dealt with properly, we are susceptible to getting them met in an unhealthy or ungodly way. Many victims I have worked with through the years have found themselves seeking emotional fulfillment outside their own marriage relationship. Sometimes it ends in an affair, other times it is what Lois Mowday calls in her book, *The Snare,* "an emotional entanglement." She comments in her book that often people who suffer emotional pain are particularly susceptible to having affairs or entanglements outside their marriage. She quotes three primary sources of emotional pain: (1) lack of self-worth; (2) lack of intimacy with others, or loneliness; and (3) lack of intimacy with God.

> Lack of self-worth is a fertile field for immorality to take root. If we are feeling bad about ourselves, and a person comes along who is not only sympathetic but also builds up our damaged ego, look out. It is only natural to be drawn to warm and caring compliments. These compliments are not an authentic measure of our self-worth, but we are unable to evaluate that truth in light of our pain. All we know is that we feel bad and that being with this certain person makes us feel good.[1]

I have counseled many men and women who found themselves in the midst of a relationship they had no intention of beginning, but because of deep, previously unmet needs, they were vulnerable.

There was a time, early in our marriage and soon after Heather was born, that I was in that kind of vulnerable situation. I had gone from a career woman to a full-time homemaker. I loved being at home, but became somewhat depressed due to a lack of stimulating conversation and to our tight financial situation. I had no idea at that time that my self-worth was so damaged. I had covered it over very well by my job and other accomplishments.

RECOGNIZING VULNERABILITY

I was just beginning to look at some of the hurts of my past when Don and I met a police lieutenant whom we had contacted regarding trespassing of some youngsters on our property. The lieutenant was an older man who was very sympathetic to our problem, and he sat down with us in his office to discuss the matter. As I sat there, I noticed he was especially attentive to me, but I thought nothing more about it after we left.

About three days later, the lieutenant showed up at

our front door. He was "in the area" and thought he would check up on the trespassing situation. I invited him in and we had a brief, informal conversation. During this time he was complimentary and commented on how enjoyable it was to talk to me. We talked of our families, and I even shared my faith with him. I talked freely about being a Christian and what that meant. When he left that day, I felt a little twinge of uneasiness, but I rationalized it away, thinking I was taking all this too personally.

I shared with Don later that evening about the visit and Don did not seem to be alarmed, so it just confirmed that everything was all right.

The following week the lieutenant called just to see how I was. I knew something was not right, but he seemed very genuine and I enjoyed our chats.

Later that week he showed up at my door again. This time the conversation was more personal. He wasn't particularly happy in his marriage and at times the pressures of his job got to him. I felt uncomfortable that day. I found myself eating up his attentiveness and his seemingly genuine appreciation for my intellect and personality. He was so complimentary that it became awkward. I continued to bring the Lord into the conversation and even said to him that it sounded like his heart was hungry for a relationship with God. When he left, I knew this was not right. Even though I had no impure motives, my need to receive affirmation was feeding on something unhealthy and ungodly.

I began to pray and realized I must put a stop to these encounters. There was a part of me that didn't want to stop because some deep needs in me were being met. Don was no longer impressed by my intellect, wit or personality as this man seemed to be. Don seemed too busy to communicate with me about issues other than, "What's for dinner?"

I knew I was particularly vulnerable, and I decided I must "abstain from all appearance of evil" (1 Thessalonians 5:22, KJV).

The next time the lieutenant phoned, I made it clear that it was not all right for him to drop over unless Don was home. I invited him to attend church with us and encouraged his pursuit of a relationship with God. I never heard from him again.

I see now how my neediness was fertile ground. By God's grace I did not pursue this. Many who find themselves in the middle of these situations cannot see the danger before it is too late. If you are in a situation like this right now, FLEE. Remember, the "enemy walks around like a roaring lion, seeking whom he may devour" (1 Peter 5:8). Don't let the temporary satisfaction of a fleeting relationship rob you of God's best. Go to the root and allow the Holy Spirit to repair the damage of your heart and to heal you!

We must seek to insulate our relationships with a protective shield that cannot be penetrated by outside forces. Prayer is one protection, obedience is another. As we commit ourselves to persistent prayer and obedience, our relationships will stand firm through the storms of life.

We have looked at insulating our relationships and at being aware of our susceptibility to outside influences. Now, what about isolation? What is the difference between insulation and isolation?

ISOLATION

Isolation carries the idea of being separate from others. In most Christian circles this separation has a positive connotation. We are to be "in the world, but not of the world" (John 17:16). There is a set-apartness that should be distinctive about us as believers. There is, however, a danger when the separation becomes more like a quarantine, a forced state of isolation.

A Closed Family System

Although my parents were quite active in our church while I was growing up, a certain isolationism permeated our home. I was not allowed to have friends over much, nor was I allowed to visit other friends' homes. I did go away to church camp, but it seemed as I got older, the reins tightened instead of loosening. My parents socialized with a few friends, but most of them were not committed Christians. The "wall" around our home could not be penetrated. My stepdad scrutinized all contact and was rigid about my relationships.

This is often characteristic of a dysfunctional family and is known as a "closed family system." The members of the family keep family secrets and do not seek outside help. There is a subtle inference that everything "out there" is bad, and betrayal of the family is unthinkable.

The Church's Part

Unfortunately, besides families, many churches set up this type of isolation mentality. Members are dissuaded from going "out of the fellowship" for any type of assistance concerning marriage or family problems. Many fine churches offer counseling services, support groups and crisis intervention, and those are excellent resources to be utilized. The danger comes when those in leadership discourage or even "forbid" members from disclosing their private family issues to outsiders. I have encountered this many times, especially when sexual abuse is occurring in the home. Church members are told to keep this information to themselves, and the church, with little knowledge of what the course of action needs to be, tries to assist the family.

I once had a call from a dear pastor who said to me, "I have just found out that one of our thirteen-year-old girls has been sexually molested by her adult brother. Her parents became aware of the situation and brought the son and daughter both in to me for counseling. The adult son is obviously deeply repentant. While they were here he sobbed about what happened. I told the parents I was sure, since the young man felt so bad about it, it would never happen again, and I sent them all home. Now I wonder, is there anything else that I should tell them?"

I answered the pastor, "I have no doubt the young man was sincere in his repentance, but the family really needs on-going help." I reviewed the laws in California with him, and then said, "According to law, you are a mandated reporter. That means you are liable and could be sued if you have information about a minor being abused and fail to report it to Child Protective Services in your county." Then I asked, "How long has this been going on in that family?"

He answered, "The girl says six years."

I explained to him, "These things do not just go away, and I urge you to report it."

He said, "I am their pastor, and I do not want to violate the confidence of this family. Since they came to me, I am concerned that they would feel I had betrayed them."

"My experience," I replied, "plus my research, has taught me that the abuse will only continue."

He promised to keep seeing the family and try to monitor what was going on.

About six months went by and I happened to call this pastor regarding another matter. Then I asked, "Whatever happened to the family we discussed a few months ago?"

Hesitantly, he told me, "The family saw me two or three times, then decided everything was fine. They ended up moving to another community near here, and the last I heard, the girl, now fourteen, was pregnant (probably by her brother) and the family was considering an abortion."

I could tell by the pastor's response that he was grieved. I was grieved, too.

BREAKING THE CYCLE

I have received hundreds of phone calls and letters through the last several years from victims who mistakenly thought the abuse was limited to what happened to them twenty years ago. In an effort to demonstrate their forgiveness toward their perpetrator, or out of convenience, they have exposed their children to that person. They have allowed the perpetrator to care for the children, or have remained silent about their own victimization while watching as the offender cares for other family members' children. The cycle is repeated over and over. Exodus 34:7*b* says the sins of the fathers are visited "upon the children and the children's children to the third and fourth generation." Numerous studies support this "curse" of the generations.

This is not meant to be a message of doom, but of hope. I believe God is bringing out the issues of victimization and dysfunctional family systems because awareness is the first step in breaking the generational curse. Only through the power of the Holy Spirit can this bondage be broken, but only as we bring these hurts into the light can we give God access to them so He can touch and heal them.

Don and I have committed ourselves to breaking unhealthy patterns in our lives so we will not pass them on to our children. We are not perfect parents, but we have experienced much healing, and it has produced a healthier environment for our girls. Being a victim of some type of dysfunctional home does not mean you are destined to be an abuser, but you must allow for the possibility that your foundation may be faulty and need attention.

I continue to pray Isaiah 54:13 over my children on a regular basis. It says: "All your children shall be taught by the LORD, and great shall be the peace of your children." We must do our part to insulate our marriage and family from destructive outside influences. We also must avoid an isolationism that allows the secret sins to continue. And finally, we must give ourselves to the work of the Holy Spirit as He desires to "bring us into all truth" (John 16:13) and break the yoke of bondage in our lives.

10

*Is the Roof Leaking?
–Don*

We bought our home in 1984. It was eighteen years old and it still had its original wooden shingle roof. It never occurred to me to pay much attention to the roof—it looked good from the street, and there were no indications of water damage when we walked through our house.

After one of our Southern California windstorms, though, we found some of the shingles from our roof on the driveway, and the ones the wind had not blown off were badly weather-beaten and warped on the ends. *A new roof would be nice,* I thought, *but I'm not convinced we need one yet. Besides, it would be expensive.*

During one of our infrequent rainstorms, however, I discovered some real problems. It had rained steadily for two days, and I was in my youngest daughter Kellie's room singing her to sleep when I noticed a water spot on her ceiling.

This man with a mission got out his flashlight, bucket and ladder. No way was my daughter going to sleep in a bedroom with a leaky ceiling! I climbed into the attic, and I heard the drip, drip, drip of the water. Aiming my trusty flashlight toward the area of the sound, I saw it — standing water and soaked insulation, right above Kellie's ceiling. Over the studs and insulation I crawled. Sure enough, the old, worn-out shingles had split, making a small opening in the roof.

First, I removed the drenched insulation; then I sponged up the standing water. We were fortunate the ceiling hadn't caved in at that spot — the water had created so much additional weight.

I balanced my bucket on a two-by-four under the hole and climbed down from the attic. That night I had to empty the bucket twice, and then once more before I went to work the next morning.

As a father I was upset at what could have happened to Kellie had the ceiling fallen in while she slept, and I was motivated to correct the problem. We put on an entire new roof as soon as we could. I provided the covering my family needed.

My friend, Gene, who owns a roofing company, told me the roof is the most important part of the structure of a house.

"It is a cover that protects everything," he said. "Water is the major problem; it can destroy everything in the structure."

ATTITUDE LEAKS

As Gene explained the importance of a strong, well-maintained roof, I thought about my experience with the leaky roof, and how important we husbands are in the protection or covering of our wives and children. We read in 1 Corinthians 11:3: "I want you to know that the head of every man is Christ, the head of woman is man, and the head of Christ is God." God has ordained a "headship" or covering to which we are accountable, and to which we may go for shelter and protection. This is what I am to be to my wife and children. I am not just to be the leader, or the final "authority" on issues. I am to create an environment of safety and protection that "covers" my family through the storms of life.

When victims marry, the husband's attitude plays a significant role in the recovery process. If, like a roof, he maintains an attitude of support and protection, the inside of the house is secure. If he adopts a distant, discouraging attitude, he no longer provides the necessary shelter, and the roof begins to leak, causing damage inside the home.

In talking with many men through the last six years, I have discovered a number of attitude leaks that men have assumed when their wives have been victims. The first attitude leak is *ignorance*. The second is *denial*. The third is *projecting blame*, and the fourth is an attitude leak of *non-support*. Let's look more closely at these attitude leaks and then discuss the patchwork that needs to be done to repair them.

Attitude Leak #1 — Ignorance

When Jan and I began our journey through the recovery process in 1981, I had no knowledge of victimization. I had a difficult time believing that events like what Jan described actually took place. It was even more difficult to believe that the past could have such a major impact on a person later in life. Like many husbands, I had an attitude leak of ignorance.

The following letters are samples of the mail we receive daily. I include them here to help you understand the magnitude of the problem as well as to validate your own wife's experience.

Dear Jan,

To begin, I am a newlywed. I have been married less than two years and I have two children. My son is from a previous relationship but my hus-

band has really been a good father to both
children. Our marriage was doing very well for a
while, but then I began to have problems being intimate with my husband, and I began to have
nightmares. I had told my husband about the incident before we were married but neither of us had
any idea how it would affect our marriage.

I'm sure you know this isn't an easy thing to
write about. I have told only one other person besides my husband, but I have been trying very
hard to forget the whole thing. I know that is not
possible. I have forgiven my stepfather a hundred
times in my heart, but it doesn't make it any less
painful. You see, I loved and trusted my stepfather.

Please send me any information that you can. I
need to save my marriage and my sanity.

Dear Jan,

I'm writing you very much in need of your
prayers. You know how being molested damages,
so you can understand. I'm trying to trust the
Lord so much, and yet it's so hard when you've
blocked so much out and it's being revealed . . .
The depression has worsened. There are suicidal
feelings three or more times a week . . . I'm still
holding on to what little hope there is.

I remembered having my dad's baby and
taking care of it, and then having the baby taken
away from me. This house where they used me for
pornography keeps coming back — and the base-
ment where they cut on me, burnt me, and put
knives up me. Jan, I felt it my responsibility to
write to you and ask if it's okay for me to have a
hate so great for them . . . The nightmares and in-
somnia are overwhelming, and then there are days
when I don't feel at all — I feel so shut off, and I
have to confess, I have so great an anger at them
that I'd like to kill them. It wasn't okay as a child

*to get angry or hate . . . I'm trying to combat the
severe depression, fear, guilt and anger, and at
times it feels hopeless. I've begged and pleaded
with God and yet can't seem to understand why.
Does God really understand the humongous hate
I have for them? Is it okay for me to feel this way
toward them? Throughout all of this, I keep seeking Him, but it seems He's so far away . . .*

As you can tell by reading these letters, there is a
great deal a victim of sexual abuse does not understand, herself. It is confusing, frustrating and frightening, all at the
same time. Many husbands demonstrate their attitude leak
of ignorance by not acquainting themselves with the common symptoms of victimization. When issues arise, they are
caught off guard and have little understanding of where the
present problem is rooted.

One significant symptom that gets most men's attention is the sexual disinterest on the part of their wives. It
should come as no surprise that a person who has been
sexually abused may have difficulties in this intimate area.
A man needs to understand that his wife's disinterest may
have little to do with him, and everything to do with working through the pain of her past. Sometimes the wife is as
frustrated over her inability to respond as the husband is.

Another symptom that particularly affected our relationship was Jan's anger. Early in our marriage, it seemed
Jan was angry with me most of the time. Her anger came
out at me in the form of extremely critical comments. No
matter how hard I tried, I could not please her. Coming from
an alcoholic home, one of the few ways I received positive
strokes was through performance. In order to get attention,
I did well in school and athletics. Performance became crucial to my self-esteem.

The problems seemed to compound. When our sexual relationship was not good I began to blame myself. I was
not "performing" well. I thought that if Jan had difficulty

relating intimately with me, there must be some deficiency in me. I tried harder in other areas, only to be hit with Jan's relentless criticism over simple things. I remember the anxiety and pressure I felt driving the car when Jan was with me. I had to make sure I was going the right direction, the right speed and to the right place, to avoid her criticisms. One day we drove to the mall, and I remember thinking, *Oh, my gosh, there are three thousand parking places here and I've got to choose the "right" one.*

Many men display the attitude leak of ignorance in that they believe they are the only couple having to work through these issues. The uneducated husband believes the problems resulting from abuse are rare and affect only his own wife negatively.

Some conservative studies estimate that at least one in four women in this country has been sexually molested by the time she is eighteen. Some say the figure is closer to 40 percent. We are not trying to sensationalize this issue, but we do not want to minimize it, either. We believe it has been a much-overlooked issue in the breakdown of marital relationships.

In *Healing of Memories,* David Seamands says,

> In March 1983, Karl Meninger, the respected
> elder statesman of psychiatrists, said that in the
> United States, incest is becoming almost as com-
> mon as shoplifting.[1]

The problem is much more widespread than we think, even in Christian homes.

As Jan mentioned in the last chapter, Exodus says the sins of the father will be passed down through several generations. Incest is generational. I believe the greatest legacy we, as husbands and fathers, can leave our families is to stop the cycle of these generational sins. The husband who has an attitude leak of ignorance is not equipped to patch that leak.

Attitude Leak #2 — Denial

The second attitude leak common in husbands of abuse victims is the denial of their own dysfunctional or deprived background. Most husbands see the problems in their marriage as caused by their wife's history of abuse. I had this same attitude and thought that once Jan "got fixed," our relationship would be great. It was convenient for me to blame our marital difficulties on Jan's past. It made it easier to deny I had any problems.

We have found that victims tend to marry victims. We find also that spouses of victims who were sexually abused usually fall into four categories:

One, they were sexually, physically or emotionally abused themselves.

Two, they grew up in an alcoholic home or a dry alcoholic home.

Three, they grew up in a rigid, oftentimes "religious" home.

Four, they came from an emotionally deprived home.

Many times persons who grew up in Christian homes grew up in what appeared to be a good environment. Sometimes families in these homes are provided with material indications of love but the children grow up emotionally starved for nurturing. For example, Jan gave a seminar on parenting once and asked the audience how they knew they were loved as children. One man immediately raised his hand and said, "I knew I was loved because my parents provided a home, food and clean clothes for me to wear."

Although as parents, we do provide those things for our children because we love them, there are very few children who lie in bed at night listening to the washing machine running and say to themselves, "I know my mom and dad love me, because right now Mom is washing my clothes."

Children need more than that. They need appropriate affection, affirmation and love that communicates to *their* hearts. All of us have our own special "language of love." Part of our job as a spouse and a parent is to find out how we can best convey that love to the other person.

Many husbands refuse to accept responsibility for their role in any marriage difficulties. I came from a dysfunctional alcoholic home. It wasn't until Jan and I were almost six years into our marriage that I honestly looked at how my growing up in that environment had affected our marriage.

Often husbands are so caught up in their "wife's problem" that their total focus is on telling her how she can get healed, even to the point of trying to do some of her recovery work. This is codependency. In her book, *Please Don't Say You Need Me,* Jan Silvious states:

> Codependent relationships form between a weak and a strong person. The strong person, the codependent, has a need to be needed, to be leaned upon, to help. The weak person, the emotionally dependent, is needy, wants to lean and to be helped. Both feel better when they operate within these roles. Each one feels good when he or she is joined with the other in a relationship. Yet it requires so much emotional energy to perpetuate this arrangement that the two people often have little time left for other relationships.[2]

Attitude Leak #3 — Blaming

Many husbands are so ignorant of the effects of incest and so out of touch with their own dysfunctional background that the third attitude leak begins to appear. This is the leak of blaming. When we were struggling in our relationship, it was convenient for me to focus the blame on Jan — after all, she was the one who had been victimized. If she didn't respond to me sexually, it was her fault. If she was critical or angry about something, it was her fault. By pushing out the blame, it allowed me to focus on her and not deal with issues in me. Unfortunately, many times husbands adopt a silent attitude that says, *This is all your fault. If you'd get fixed, we'd be fine.*

Attitude Leak #4 — Nonsupport

The last major attitude leak is that of nonsupport. This attitude is a culmination of the three previous attitudes. The husband who maintains his attitude of ignorance, denial and blaming cannot help but create an atmosphere of nonsupport. He has tremendous difficulty understanding the necessity of looking into past issues, and he really believes that if the wife would just "tough it out," everything would be fine. What husbands do not realize is that this nonsupportive stance recreates for a wife the same type of environment she experienced in childhood. It often compounds the already existing problems and tends to promote more distancing by the wife for her own protection.

What then can we as men do to repair the leaks in our attitudes? Simply stated, we can plug the leak of ignorance with *education*. We can repair the leak of denial by honestly *examining ourselves* and taking appropriate action. The attitude leak of blaming can be patched by *learning to empathize* with our wives. And finally, we can seal the leak of nonsupport by *encouraging* our wives in recovery.

EDUCATE

Husbands can begin to plug the leak of ignorance by educating themselves as much as possible. When Jan started her recovery process, there weren't many books out on the subject. Thankfully, that has changed. I have done a great deal of reading about growing up in an alcoholic family. We have provided a suggested reading list for you at the back of this book. Read all you can to educate yourself, and be willing to seek outside help. As you become more educated, you will be better equipped to handle some of the situations that inevitably will arise.

One of the incidents we were able to work through because of the knowledge we had gained was the time I unwittingly put on the same kind of aftershave lotion Jan's stepfather had used, which Jan has told you about earlier in the book. Although this was an unpleasant experience for both of us, I know now that a flashback can be a positive sign indicating a step in the direction of healing.

Often, husbands who have not educated themselves will respond to these flashbacks and to other symptoms negatively. It is important for husbands to familiarize themselves with common symptoms so they are prepared to respond in support when issues come to the surface.

EXAMINE

You can start to repair the attitude leak of denial by examining yourself. Although I knew I had some difficulties because of growing up in an alcoholic family, I denied that my background interfered in any way with our life now as a couple. A husband needs to take his focus off his wife and begin to "examine himself."

One of the best things I did to learn more about myself was to attend a support group at my church for adult children of alcoholics (ACA). Although I had spoken on the subject and had read many books, I had not been exposed to others like me in a group setting. It was astonishing to see more than a hundred people attending this weekly group. I gave myself time to get comfortable in this setting, which took about four weeks, and I began to feel a kinship with the people there. They knew what it was like to grow up in an alcoholic family. I was able to share with others, and I felt accepted. As I listened to others, I saw some of the very same patterns in my own life. For the first time, I was really able to connect some of my unhealthy patterns to my background. I realized I had issues to work on myself.

If you are an ACA, or if you were abused in childhood, or if you were traumatized by the death or abandonment of a parent, I strongly urge you to get into a support group, or to get some individual counseling. As you focus on and work through your own issues, you will see positive changes in your relationship with your wife.

I began to see how difficult it was for me to share my inner feelings with Jan. This came from never being encouraged to have feelings as a child, and it definitely affected the closeness in our relationship. As I realized my own responsibility and began to develop new, healthier ways of relating with Jan, I discovered that she was more able and willing to respond in return.

EMPATHIZE

The attitude leak of blaming can be patched by empathizing with your wife. Empathy encompasses a sincere desire to understand coupled with a genuine compassion for someone's feelings and condition. Shortly after our first daughter Heather was born, Jan became aware that she had the potential of abusing our new baby. She came to me and asked if I would support her in obtaining counseling. At this point in my life, I wouldn't even say the word "incest," much less admit that my wife was a victim of it. I was anti-counseling and saw no need for anyone to be in therapy. I came from a coach's mentality that says if you're injured, you tape it up and get back in the game. When Jan came to me and said that she felt our future depended on her getting some help, I didn't quite understand. I also had trouble with the financial aspect of her getting help, since I knew insurance would not cover counseling.

I could, however, see that Jan was in pain. I could empathize with pain. I was seriously hurt once while playing high school football. As a result of my injury, I had undergone two spinal surgeries by the time I was twenty-five. Legally, I am still 20 percent disabled, and I have endured daily pain and discomfort since my second operation. To look at me, you would think I am fine. I look healthy and fit on the outside, but my legs are plagued with constant numbness. I walk with a slight limp, and the bottoms of my feet sting as if someone were pinching them.

Jan was in pain in much the same way. Although she looked fine on the outside, inside was a hurt and emotionally disabled little girl. God used my own experience with pain to help me understand what Jan must be feeling. I knew that if I went to Jan with a plan to see a specialist for my back, she would be behind me 100 percent. She would support my attempt to relieve some of my daily pain. I could do no less for her. I didn't understand the depth of her pain or why she couldn't get over it on her own, but I supported her anyway. In empathizing with your wife, be aware that she needs your understanding that all of this was not her fault. It was not her decision to be molested or otherwise abused. So often victims are made to feel guilty by the perpetrator—"Had she not worn those cute little white shorts . . ."; or, "If she had not climbed up into Uncle Henry's lap, this never would have happened." Your wife does not need for you to add to her false sense of responsibility.

In order to empathize, it is important that you know that during the recovery process, things will get worse before they get better. Old, infected wounds will have to be opened and exposed. As the wounds are opened, your wife will be in a great deal of pain, which certainly will affect you in some ways. This is not pleasant at the time, but it must be done if healing is to take place.

The summer after Jan started counseling, we rented a vacation condominium at one of my all-time favorite spots, Lake Tahoe. We planned a week of relaxation and fun as a family. Lake Tahoe is truly one of God's most magnificent creations and is so very romantic.

The first night we were there, Jan responded to my kiss with, "Don't kiss me; don't touch me. You repulse me!"

What a guy I must be! I thought to myself.

I knew right then it was going to be a strained week, and I withdrew from Jan emotionally and physically. I felt like leaving her right then and there.

I'm glad I didn't.

As you and your wife begin this long process, take heart. Things do get better. You must be committed and prepared to give it time. Recovery from an abusive past is not easy. You can't undo in twenty-four sessions of counseling what has accumulated over twenty-four years. It takes time and work. We have reaped the benefits and have seen God's promise in Jeremiah 30:17 come to pass: " 'For I will restore health to you and heal you of your wounds,' says the LORD."

I do not regret my supportive stance nor the financial investment. Jan and I now regard that as one of the best investments we ever made. We experience more love and closeness than I ever thought possible. It has been worth it.

ENCOURAGE

The last major roof repair is sealing the attitude leak of nonsupport. This can best be done by encouragement.

As an athletic coach I know the value of encouragement. Some seasons I have run out of ideas that would help my team perform better, and at those times of disappointment and disillusionment I call my best friend, Rod, in Boise, Idaho.

A former player of mine, and a coach himself now, Rod knows me and understands what it is like to coach. He knows how tough it is for a coach to go through a bad season. Just a few encouraging words like, "You're doing the right thing"; or, "Hang in there," can put things into perspective for me and make the season go better. There are times when I need to be sensitive to the emotions of the athletes and provide encouragement and inspiration. Athletes need to know they are appreciated and there is someone rooting for them no matter what the score is. Wives are no different.

As you begin to encourage your wife, you will find that owning your recovery as a couple will help. In our marriage seminars, I tell men they need to be committed to their wife's recovery. To illustrate this point, I use the old coach's story about what it means to be committed rather than just involved. The difference is like the ham and egg breakfast they had this morning. The chicken was *involved* in that breakfast, but the pig was *committed!* This is the kind of sacrifice we must make.

If we are truly committed to our wife's recovery and to the improvement of the marriage relationship, we will give our lives to it. If we are just involved, we will go only so far, and we will stop at the first sign of personal inconvenience or pain. Ephesians 5:24 tells us: "Husbands, love your wives, just as Christ also loved the church and gave Himself for it." Giving myself up for my wife has not always been easy for me — especially in the area of sex.

There were times in the early recovery process when Jan needed space. It was difficult for her to enter into the intimacy of the sexual union. During that time it was tough for me to keep from being resentful. I found a verse that helped, though — Colossians 3:19 (NASB): "Husbands, love your wives, and do not be embittered against them." It is often easy for a husband to become impatient when the sexual relationship is not all he envisions.

What can a husband do to help? I believe one of the most important elements a husband can build into the relationship is trust. Can your wife trust that you have her best interests at heart? Or are you looking out for yourself and making sure your needs are being met, first and foremost?

Do an experiment for two weeks. Chart the times and places you make any kind of physical contact with your wife. Look at any patterns. Does most of your touching occur in the bedroom? Does it center around *your* desire to be intimate with her? How much time are you investing in communicating on a deep, emotional level with her? Do you have a hidden agenda when you come in from work and give her a big hug and a kiss? If you do, she can probably sense it and, if you have not invested in building trust in the relationship, you can probably anticipate resistance.

One of the first things you can do to build trust is to give your wife the option when it comes to lovemaking. Remember, she had no choice in being a victim. She needs to know you will still love her even if she says no.

Another way to build trust is to have times of caressing and holding outside the bedroom. When you do this, it is important to communicate that you are not "setting her up" for later on. Sometimes I will put my arms around Jan in the kitchen and simply say, "No strings attached." She knows me well enough by now to know when I really mean that. A lot of times at night we just hold each other in bed and agree not to make love. This has allowed Jan to trust that I would follow through with what I had said, and that I wasn't trying to trick her.

As I have been able to empathize with Jan's experience, communicate my genuine love for her as a person, and encourage her in the recovery process, we have grown closer and closer together.

Let me now take a moment to encourage you as husbands. In every basketball game there is a time in the last five minutes when the game is either won or lost. We call this the "gut" of the game. Usually the team that is behind will make its final run, attempting to get ahead. If they are unsuccessful in their attempt, they normally quit trying. We refer to this as "giving in to the game." We constantly tell our team, "DON'T GIVE IN TO THE GAME." It goes something like this: We are down 13 points with five minutes left. We begin to make our run. We cut the lead to five points.

Right then, our opponent hits six straight points. We are now down by eleven. What do we do? The choice is simple. Either we start another run at them continuing to play hard, or we give in to the game. If we give in, we have no chance of victory. We must not give in. The Scripture that has been the most helpful to me is Galatians 6:9, which says: "And let us not grow weary while doing good, for in due season we shall reap if we do not lose heart."

Husbands, don't give in. Keep doing what is right. Victory is close if you stay with the game plan.

We are told in 1 Peter 3:7:

> Likewise you husbands, dwell with them with understanding, giving honor to the wife, as to the weaker vessel, and as being heirs together of the grace of life, that your prayers may not be hindered.

Have you checked your roof lately? Do you have an attitude leak of ignorance, denial, blaming or nonsupport? Or are you dwelling with your wife in an understanding way? As you repair your attitude leaks with education, examination, empathy and encouragement, you will provide a secure covering for your wife and your marriage. It will be a place of safety and a refuge from the storms of life — for both of you.

11

Homeowners' Insurance

It was summer vacation time, and I had just turned eighteen. I would start college in the fall and was working full-time as a waitress to save money for my tuition and expenses. My parents were planning a summer vacation back to the Midwest, but I didn't want to go. "Besides," I told them, "I have to work."

They were somewhat reluctant to leave me at home for the two weeks, but I promised that my friend, Lauren, would stay there part of the time.

I couldn't believe it! I would have the whole house to myself. I could keep my own hours and would not have to check in and out. It was going to be great.

I assured my parents that all would be fine and off they went. Lauren came over that night and we stayed up until all hours, watching T.V. and eating junk food. We went to work, to the beach, shopping; we played tennis, and we had a great time.

One evening, when my parents had been gone about a week, we decided to go out for a while after work. We finally got in about midnight. Lauren wanted to shower before we went to bed, so she went into my bathroom and I went to use my parents' bathroom. I stepped onto the carpet and instantly felt it slosh. The entire carpet was drenched.

At first, I couldn't figure out what had happened. Lauren was out of the shower by this time and I called to her. I looked in my parents' shower stall—it was totally backed up, and overflowing with putrid water. I went to the garage and got a couple of buckets and we started bailing.

That bathroom was in the back of the house, so we had to carry those buckets of water through the house to dump them out in front. It was past midnight and we were in our nighties—and the humor of it all struck. We started laughing uncontrollably. What would the neighbors say if they looked out and saw these two young girls in their scanty nighties, emptying buckets of water in the planter off the front porch?

Eventually, the shower stall was empty. Next, we had to deal with the carpeting. We got down on our hands and knees and began ripping it up. Fortunately, the bathroom was quite small, so there was not much there. The problem was, it was saturated—and extremely heavy. We got part of it free and tried to pick it up, but even for the two of us it was tough. Our hysterical laughter didn't help. When we finally managed to pick it up and started to carry it out of the bathroom, we noticed little streams of water running from it onto the other carpet, so we ran the rest of the way to get it to the garage as fast as we could. We did the same thing with the pad. We went to bed that night, afraid to use any plumbing because we weren't sure what else might happen.

The next day I went to my parents' safe, got out their homeowners' insurance policy and called their agent to notify him of what had happened. He told me to keep track of all the costs involved and said they would replace the carpeting if it was beyond being salvaged. I called a plumbing service and they came out that afternoon and roto-rooted the line. I also called a carpet cleaning service to come out and clean the rest of the carpet.

After everything was taken care of, I called my parents to let them know what happened. I think they were shocked.

"How did you know who to call?" asked my mom.

"Well, I looked in the safe for your insurance policy and it listed your agent," I said rather proudly.

My stepdad got on the phone and said they'd take care of the rest when they got home.

I was quite impressed with myself and so were my parents, and we all were thankful for the insurance.

Here in California, a homeowner is required by law to have homeowners' insurance if there is a loan on the property. That insurance protects the lender's investment even though, once you move into the home, the lender has no say as to how you keep up the house so long as you keep up the payments. The insurance provides uniform coverage for things like personal contents, liability, additional living expenses if your house burns down and you must stay in a hotel, guest medical coverage, and worker's compensation.

Of course, homeowners hope they never will have to utilize their policies, but they appreciate having them when the need arises. The insurance cannot prevent the damage, but it can provide coverage and compensation when they suffer loss.

In a marriage, our homeowners' insurance is prayer. Prayer cannot prevent certain tragedies from occurring, but it can cover us when the storms of life hit. In Matthew 18:7 Jesus warns: "Woe to the world because of offenses! For offenses must come, but woe to that man by whom the offense comes!" Jesus recognized that we will suffer offenses in this life, often at the hands of others.

Then He encouraged us in John 16:33 when He said, "These things I have spoken to you, that in Me you may have peace. In the world you will have tribulation; but be of good cheer, I have overcome the world."

We have seen in reading thus far that God has a design for marriage that is good. We have shared how our faulty foundations and contaminated soil can fracture our relationship. We have discussed the steps of pouring a new foundation and building a structurally sound marriage relationship. Now we need to look at some outside events that can rob us of the joy and unity God intended us to experience in marriage.

CRITTERS IN THE ATTIC

About six months after we had moved into our home, I began hearing noises on the roof at night. I thought there must be some cats on the prowl in the neighborhood.

Then one day while preparing dinner, I got some potatoes from my cupboard and noticed small holes in several of them. I tossed them out and thought nothing more about it. A few days later, while cleaning a dishtowel drawer in my kitchen, I noticed some "droppings." I cringed as I thought about what this meant. I called to Don and said, "Do you remember when I told you about the noise on the roof the other night?"

"Yes," he replied, coming into the kitchen.

"Well, I don't think it was a cat. I think we have mice up there. The other day I discovered some potatoes with little holes in them, and now look in this drawer."

Don looked, wrinkled up his nose, and said, "You'd better call someone."

I could not get to the phone fast enough. The exterminators came out that very day. I told them I had been hearing sounds and that I was sure we had mice. One of the men looked in the dishtowel drawer and said rather matter-of-factly, "Ma'am, you don't have mice; you have rats."

I thought I would die right then and there. I began to shiver with disgust.

"How can you tell?" I asked.

"When you're in this business as long as I've been," he said quite proudly with a Southern drawl, "you get to know the droppin's. These here are definitely from rats. If you had mice, these droppin's would be only half this size. Yup, I'd say the critters you got are 'bout this size." He held up his hands and measured off about 12 inches in length, then added, "Not countin' the tail, o'course."

"Of course," I said, and I sat down at the kitchen table to keep from passing out.

"What do we do to get rid of them?" I asked, still feeling squeamish.

"We'll go take a look up in the attic and set out some poison. It'll take about a week for 'em to die. Then we'll come out again just to make sure."

After inspecting the attic, Barney, with whom I was now on a first-name basis, came down and said, "You sure do have some big ones up there, Ma'am."

"Did you see them?" I asked in horror.

"Ah, no. Them critters are more afraid of us than we are of them. I could just tell from the paths they made through your insulation. Now don't you worry; we laid out the poison in several different spots. They'll be dead in no time."

I was afraid to ask the next question, but could hold it in no longer. "What happens after they die? Are they just going to lie up there?"

"No, Ma'am," Barney said confidently. "Y'see, the kind of poison we put out makes 'em real thirsty. They eat the poison, and then go try to find water. Once they're out of the attic, they usually die before they can get back in."

Barney assured me he would be back in about ten days to check the attic and remove "anything" that had not found its way out.

I could barely go into my kitchen. Barney had explained that the rats must have gotten thirsty and climbed down the walls into my kitchen cupboards and helped themselves to my potatoes. Although it had been at least three days since I handled those potatoes, I immediately went to the sink and washed my hands.

As the nights passed, I heard less and less activity. Finally, the pitter-pattering stopped. The exterminators came out again, and all was well.

CHANGING PROBLEM PATTERNS

When victims marry, each mate brings vulnerable spots into the marriage relationship—sensitivities, habit patterns and weaknesses which are the result of outside influences—"critters in their attics." These outside events have caused individual instability and insecurity. The circumstances of life cannot always be controlled, but our responses to those circumstances can. The first step in warding off the problems caused by these patterns is recognition.

RECOGNITION

How do we recognize our vulnerabilities? We try to become aware of the areas in which we get hurt or caught unaware repeatedly.

One night following a basketball game, I asked Don why all his players taped up different areas of their bodies.

"They've learned, honey, where their areas of vulnerability are. When you play the game long enough, you find your weak spots because those are where you get injured the easiest," he answered. "Most basketball players tape their ankles because they need the extra support in that area. Have you noticed that some players wear a knee brace?"

"Yes. Is it because they're already hurt?"

"Sometimes, but many times their knees are their vulnerable spots, so they just take precautions."

"What would happen if all your players decided not to tape their ankles or knees?"

"That would be stupid. They'd just be asking for trouble."

I later reflected on that conversation and realized this concept pertains to *every* Christian, not just those who have been victimized. We must recognize our weak areas and provide proper support to avoid injury.

How is that done? Prayer, but more specifically, the spiritual warfare type of prayer. We must realize that the enemy "walks about like a roaring lion, seeking whom he may devour" (1 Peter 5:8). I am convinced the enemy knows our areas of vulnerability and will attack in those areas whenever he can. We must learn to "put on the whole armor of God" (Ephesians 6:11), and to use the Sword of the Spirit. We are told to "pray without ceasing" (1 Thessalonians 5:17).

I grew up in a fundamental church where the Bible was taught, and I heard often about God's armor: the loins girt with truth; the breastplate of righteousness; the helmet of salvation; the feet shod with the preparation of the gospel; the shield of faith; and the Sword of the Spirit. I was taught to put on the armor, but never told about using the Sword. It wasn't until I had been a Christian for more than twenty years that I found out how to fight the enemy by using that Sword, which is God's Word.

Since this subject could be an entire book by itself, I will merely encourage you to look into the area of spiritual warfare. Two of the hottest books on the market over the past few months have been Frank Peretti's books, *This*

Present Darkness and *Piercing the Darkness,* both illuminating the area of spiritual warfare.

The enemy is a robber. He cannot take away our salvation, so he tries to rob us of our joy and of the good things of God. He knows our accessible areas and he will attempt to infiltrate. He is one of the "critters in the attic."

One month short of one year after we had the exterminators out, I started to hear noises in the attic again. I couldn't believe it! They were back. At first, Don thought I was crazy, but I knew I was right. I wasted no time getting on the phone. I called the same exterminating company because they had a one-year guarantee on their work.

Barney was no longer with them, and I guessed he had moved on to bigger and better things. They sent out a couple of other men, though, and I related the story to them. One of them asked, "Did the guys seal up the holes when they were here the first time?"

"What holes?"

"Unless you seal up the holes," he explained, "every winter the rats will be back. They're looking for a warm place for shelter from the cold."

"Where are these holes you're talking about?" I asked. I didn't know of any "holes" in our house.

"Let's take a look and see."

Both men walked around our home, pointing out different areas where rats could find access to the attic. There was a small hole near the upper part of our fireplace, another one near the vent for our clothes dryer in the garage and another near the roof in the front of the house.

"You mean they can get in even through those tiny holes?" I asked.

"Yes, Ma'am. We'll put some more poison up there right now, then we'll come back in ten days and cover those holes with a special wire mesh that will prevent access."

"Why can't you just put up the wire stuff now?"

"First, we want to poison them. You see the poison makes them thirsty and . . . "

This sounded all too familiar. The men did come back ten days later, and they sealed up the holes. We have had no trouble since, with the exception of one critter that didn't make it out of the attic.

I have become familiar with my own areas of vulnerability, my own "access areas." One is in feeling inadequate and unworthy of God's love. When Satan wants to get to me, he usually attacks in this area.

When we were praying about writing this book, I kept hearing a little voice inside saying, *What makes you think you can do it again? Yeah, you've written one book, but you'll never pull another one together.* I heard that voice for months and it paralyzed me. Every time I would sit down at our computer, I'd find myself thinking those same thoughts. I asked friends to pray and I began to rebuke the lies the enemy was planting.

Because I know my vulnerability in this area, I spent considerable time memorizing Scripture that speaks of God's unconditional love and acceptance and of His adequacy and power. I used the Word of God to repel the enemy's attacks. The Scripture tells us that when we resist him, he will flee. He would flee, but usually not for long. Like the basketball player, I had to identify my weak areas and tape them up with the reinforcing support of God's Word.

RESPONSE

Sometimes we recognize an area of vulnerability but are not sure how to respond. This was true for me three years ago. I had been praying that God would show me the last issues I needed to work through in my therapy. It seemed God kept bringing up the issue of unresolved anger toward my mother. I asked my therapist if she thought this was an area I needed to work on. She responded with a definite yes. I was not too happy about her enthusiasm and said somewhat sarcastically, "I'll bet you take all your clients through this mother stuff. I'm not so convinced that all of that hasn't been taken care of already."

She and I talked about different areas where I was still a bit angry with my mother. The biggest one was my mother's lack of protection. Even when I had told my mother about the abuse, she did nothing to protect me. I knew I couldn't trust her. I told my therapist I was aware of these areas, but felt I had worked through them sufficiently. She urged me to pray and ask the Lord if there were any "roots" that needed to be pulled out. I agreed to pray.

I asked the Lord the following week to make very clear to me any unresolved hurts, anger or bitterness still there concerning my mother. He brought nothing immediately to mind.

It was springtime and Don and I were doing our couples' seminar at a church in Denver, Colorado. This trip gave us a rare opportunity — we could take our girls with us. They had never flown before, and they were excited. The seminar went well, and when we were ready to go home our friend Paul, who had organized the seminar, came to pick us up at the hotel. It had snowed while we were there, so it was very cold that Sunday morning. Paul and Don carried our five pieces of luggage out to Paul's truck. I had the girls by one hand and my briefcase containing my Bible and speaking notes in the other. As I approached the truck, I asked myself, *Should I give Don my briefcase to put in the back of the truck? Or should I keep it with me in the back seat?* I thought, *No, I'll just give it to him to load.*

The ride to the airport took about thirty minutes. On the way, Paul and I carried on an intense discussion while Don and the girls sat silent. I could tell Don was uncomfortable with the conversation, and when we got to the airport, he was out of the truck in a hurry. I said goodbye to Paul and took the girls into the terminal while Don and Paul unloaded the truck. Don came in with the luggage and we headed for the United ticket counter.

"Where is my briefcase?" I asked him.

He looked at me dumbfounded. "I don't know."

"You don't know?" I asked, rather irritated.

"No."

"Well, did you take it out of the back of the truck?"

"I don't remember."

"You don't remember? Do you remember putting it in the truck?" I asked, sharply now.

"Not particularly," Don said innocently.

By this time I was angry. I lashed out, "I handed it to you when you were loading the truck. I can't believe this!"

I did what I always do in such situations—I took control. I stomped off to find the skycap, leaving my husband there with the girls. The skycap took me to the lost luggage counter where we learned nothing had been turned in. I still did not know whether my briefcase had been unloaded, whether it was mistakenly carried off by someone else, or whether it was in Paul's truck.

I went back to Don and the girls, and I said to Don, "I can't believe you did this."

Immediately, I saw Don back up from me emotionally. He was angry, but he said, "Give me a quarter—I'll try to call Paul. You take the girls to the gate area."

We arrived at the gate area shortly after 11 A.M.; our flight would depart at noon. I sat in the waiting room, filled with rage. Why had I trusted my husband with something so important? Why hadn't I just taken it with me in the back seat? You'd think I would have learned by now. How stupid to think I could trust him! Tears filled my eyes and started running down my cheeks and I was oblivious to everything around me. My emotions ran wild. I flipped back and forth between anger and abandonment. *Why do I always have to take care of myself? Why can't I depend on Don to take care of me?*

A voice inside me said, *That's the way it's always been. Face it and live with it.*

Don came back about 11:20 and said, "Paul's not home."

My anger reared its ugly head again. "Did you call the church to see if he was there?"

"I didn't know the number."

I glared at him, thinking to myself, *Use your brain. Call information.* Aloud I said, "I'll go call. You sit with the girls." I telephoned the church and the receptionist put ushers on the alert for Paul. I stood holding the phone for about fifteen minutes. Paul was nowhere to be found.

I walked back to find Don and the girls; they were sitting in the waiting area by themselves. Everyone else had already boarded the plane. My husband took one look at me and knew I was defeated.

In desperation he said, "Let me try Paul's number one more time."

I looked at him with squinting, angry eyes and said, "Forget it. It's too late. It's gone. There's nothing you can do now."

With that we got on the plane.

As I walked down the aisle, I could not hold back the tears. Yet it seemed I heard the Lord's voice speaking to me just before I reached my seat, *Jan, you haven't even prayed about this situation.*

I settled into my seat, in front of Don, and took a deep breath. "Oh, Lord," I said, "please forgive me—it's my briefcase. My Bible, my precious Bible is in there. If You can do anything about it, Lord, would You do it for me?"

The words were barely spoken when a stewardess's voice came over the loud speaker. "Would passenger Frank please light her call button?"

I remember reaching up as if in slow motion. I peered out into the aisle and gasped when I saw a stewardess walking toward me, hugging my briefcase.

As she came nearer, the Spirit of God spoke Isaiah 65:24 to my heart: "Before they call, I will answer; and while they are still speaking, I will hear."

When the stewardess reached me I said, "Oh, my briefcase! How did it get here? Who brought it?"

She looked at me, and in all sincerity she said, "An angel brought it." (This is the absolute truth!)

I simply replied, "You don't know how true that is."

She handed me my briefcase and I took it and held it in my arms – and burst into full crying. The man across the aisle must have thought I had a million dollars in that briefcase.

I reached back to grab Don's hand and said, "Honey, I'm so sorry."

I took my Bible out and held it to my chest. The Holy Spirit began to minister to me. I could sense Him tenderly saying, *Jan, this is not a "Don issue" or even a "briefcase issue." This is a "mother issue." Your intense reaction has to do with a mother who was not there for you, a mother you could not depend on to take care of you. That is the earthly truth. The eternal and everlasting truth is that I will NEVER let you down.*

As I sat there weeping, I knew God would not always answer in such a tangible way as He did that day, but the truth of His love and utter trustworthiness was planted in my heart at that time.

I went back to therapy the next week and worked for the next six months on the issues with my mother.

Sometimes there are pockets of debris in our lives—and we are not even aware of them. Isaiah 28:29 says: "This also comes from the LORD of hosts, who is wonderful in counsel and excellent in guidance." We must recognize our weaknesses, respond with wisdom, and allow God to restore us to wholeness.

RESTORATION

God has a unique insurance plan for each of us who are His. He promises to "restore to you the years that the swarming locust has eaten" (Joel 2:25) and to "make all things new" (Revelation 21:5). His insurance plan is not limited, nor does He require a deductible. You see, His Son already paid the full price.

You may be in a marriage or a relationship that seems hopeless. You may be struggling through the intense pain of victimization, and wondering, *Where was God when all this happened?* You may fear the pain will never subside. You may feel you will never be able to trust again. If you're a husband, you even may feel victimized yourself by your wife and her experience. You may feel like just giving up. We understand how you feel. So does God.

The truth is that His heart is open to you today. Run to Him; He has all that you need.

12

Stumbling Blocks to Unity

Have you ever thought about the meaning of Psalm 133:1? It says: "Behold, how good and how pleasant it is for brethren to *dwell together in unity.*"

Most of us have not spent much time pondering what "dwell in unity" means—we just know when we're not dwelling in it. Some of the most pleasant times I have are when I watch my two little girls play in harmony with each other. When they have decided to work on a project, color, play dolls, or make plans for a "show," I am thrilled to see the enjoyment and closeness they are developing as sisters.

On the other hand, nothing is so aggravating as their bickering when each of them wants to control the other. Some days they each just seem to focus on what the other is doing, and take that one to task. It's, "Mom, Heather has the T.V. changer and its my turn to watch my show"; or, "Mom, Kellie took my purse and she won't give it back"; or, "That's no fair. You took the last piece of gum"; or, "I'm not going to play with you. You're mean." Those times are hard, but I must confess, some days I feel like acting the same way. At those times, dwelling in unity is far from my mind.

In this chapter, we will look at some of the *stumbling blocks* to unity. In Ephesians 4:1-3 Paul exhorts us:

> I, therefore, the prisoner of the Lord, beseech you to have a walk worthy of the calling with which you were called, with all lowliness and gentleness, with longsuffering, bearing with one another in love, endeavoring to keep the unity of the Spirit in the bond of peace.

Of course, unity implies a state of harmony, or peace.

STUMBLING BLOCKS TO UNITY

A few years ago I began praying about my relationship with Don concerning our unity. I asked the Lord to help us bond more closely, and to show me areas that prevented the unity of spirit I longed for. I was not prepared for what God had in store that summer.

Stumbling block #1: Unbroken ties from the past

After praying for unity in our relationship, I decided just to let God show me ways in which our unity could grow.

KEITH

One day, in June 1987, my girls and I went to spend a few days with my friend, Lauren, who lives near where I grew up. Don was out of town, visiting a friend.

On the way the Holy Spirit seemed to impress me to pray for a former boyfriend. For the whole hour's drive, I prayed for this man's salvation and for God to work in his life. I had dated Keith for nearly two years when I worked as a juvenile hall counselor. He was not a Christian, and the relationship was not particularly healthy in many ways. I was still dating him when I met Don in 1976. I broke up with Keith a few days later.

I thought it odd that Keith came to my mind that day, but figured it was due to my being in the familiar area. I had not talked to Keith in more than eight years.

When I got to my friend's house, we had a lot of fun visiting and watching the children play and swim, but Keith kept coming to my mind. At first I suspected the enemy was trying to attack me by putting this man in my thoughts while my husband was out of town. The more I considered it, though, the more impressed I was to pray. I prayed for Keith that entire day, not knowing why. The following morning was the same. By afternoon, the Lord seemed to be leading me to call Keith's house. I said, "Lord, what are You saying? Here my husband is out of town, and You first have me praying for Keith — now You want me to call him? I don't even know his number after all these years."

I thought I must be listening to the wrong voices, and I tried to resist what I was now calling a "temptation." Yet, I knew the Holy Spirit was prompting me. It was as though God were saying, *Jan, will you trust Me?*

I thought, *Lord, I hope You know what You're doing on this one!* I got out the phone book, found the number, and I said, "Okay, Lord, what do I say when I call?"

No answer.

"Okay, I'll call and see what happens."

I sat on the floor with the telephone in front of me and prayed, "Lord, I'm not sure what this is all about, but I know this is You, so please make it clear what I am to say."

I picked up the receiver and then put it down. I thought about my husband. What if he were in this situation? Would I believe him when he got home if he told me he was in a similar situation? Absolutely not!

I wavered like this for fifteen minutes, and then I sensed the Lord telling me, *Make the call. I'll tell you the rest later.* I did.

On the other end was Keith's voice — fortunately on an answering machine.

"Do I leave a message, Lord?"

I did. I simply identified myself and told Keith he had really been on my heart and that I was praying for him. I told him I didn't know what was going on, but I had learned to be obedient to God when He prompted me to pray. I hung up feeling I had done what God asked — and I was relieved.

The relief lasted just a short time, because soon the same inner "message" was prompting me to call again. I said, "No way, Lord. What else do I say?"

At that point a verse of Scripture came to mind: "Whatever you bind on earth will be bound in heaven, and whatever you loose on earth will be loosed in heaven" (Matthew 18:18).

"What does that mean, Lord?"

Tenderly, but straightforwardly, the Spirit of God ministered to my heart. He revealed to me that I had wronged Keith. I immediately resisted this because up from the recesses of my mind came the offenses Keith had committed against me. However, the Lord showed me I had held Keith accountable for things not of his doing. I had made choices in the relationship that for years I had charged to Keith's account. This, of course, was wrong, and I needed to confess that to him.

I said, "Lord, he's not even a Christian that I know of. He's not going to understand all this. Can't I just confess this to You, and then You can work in him without me getting involved?"

Again the impression on my spirit was clear: *No.*

"Okay, Lord. What do I tell him?" I asked.

You tell him exactly what I have shown you and you ask him for forgiveness.

I prayed the entire afternoon, asking God to show me where I had harbored bitterness and anger toward this man. I got into the Word and read about unforgiveness and judgment. I repented for all I had carried against Keith and asked God to release him from the bondage my judgment had imposed. I asked God to "loose" His Spirit in Keith's life, to bring him into the kingdom and to initiate revival in his heart.

I called again that evening. Again, I got the answering machine. This time I said I needed to talk to him about something and I probably would try to call again. I told him I was praying for him. I was a little puzzled. Why had the Lord so impressed my heart to call, and then have me reach only his answering machine?

Sunday, the third day, it all became clear. I spent the day with my friends and did not think about phoning Keith. I thought I had satisfied the Lord, and I prayed that God would complete His good work in Keith's life.

I drove home early that evening, put my girls in bed and settled down to wait for Don to come home. Suddenly an overwhelming thought took hold of me: *Call now.*

"Lord, Don is due home within the next hour or so." The Lord seemed to impress on me, though, that today, June 14, was significant in Keith's life, and I must reach him now.

I said, "Okay, Lord, but this is the last call. If he's not home, I'm not leaving any messages, and I'm not calling back."

I picked up the phone and dialed. Keith answered the phone—live this time. At first, I was caught off guard. Then I identified myself and said, "Keith, the Lord has had you on my heart for three days, and I have been praying for you. I have sensed there are some things going on in your life, and that especially today you needed prayer. God impressed me that this day is significant and painful for you. What happened today?" I asked.

"Interesting you should say that. I have had a rough day. It's the anniversary of my mother's death—she committed suicide fifteen years ago today. On top of that, I came home from work today and discovered my dog was dead. You're right, it has been a tough day."

I shared with him the purpose of my call. I told him I was happily married and had no intention of establishing any relationship with him, but God had been working in my heart over some issues that concerned him. I did not go into detail, but told him I had held him accountable for some things that I now realized I was responsible for. I told him I felt the bitterness I'd had toward him might have, in some way, discouraged him from being sensitive to God's leading in his own life and I wanted to ask his forgiveness. He did not understand, but I remembered that Scripture teaches, "The natural man does not receive the things of the Spirit of God, for they are foolishness to him; nor can he know them, because they are spiritually discerned" (1 Corinthians 2:14). Yet I noted a tenderness toward God in his voice. He resisted the plea for forgiveness—he saw no need. Finally, though, he graciously accepted my apology.

I closed with, "Keith, if you remember nothing else from our conversation, know that God loves you so much that He would put you on my heart after all these years. Not only that, but I believe He impressed me to call on this day in particular. He loves you, Keith. Would it be all right with you if I prayed before we hung up?"

"Yes," Keith said, "that would be nice."

I prayed that God would continue to work in Keith's life and that, above all, Keith would begin to know the love God had for him. Keith prayed too. I sensed a hunger in his heart for the Spirit of God. I may not know until eternity the impact of that day.

I told Don all about this when he came home. I was a little reluctant, not knowing how I would handle it if the situation were reversed. I did comment to Don that I felt God was not only breaking bonds in Keith's life but also in mine somehow. I wondered, *How much does this have to do with my prayer a few weeks ago for unity?*

JEANNIE

The following month, we were invited to the committee meeting for Don's twenty-year high school reunion. It would be held at Larry's home and Larry said several of Don's old buddies would be there. So would Jeannie.

Don had told me about Jeannie after we got married. He said there was nothing serious, but she was the first girl he ever had a crush on, and it was during his freshman year in high school. They never really dated, but they liked each other—and everyone knew it. When he returned to school for his sophomore year, he found out Jeannie would not be returning—she was pregnant. Don was deeply hurt. He had injured his back in football practice that summer, and it was a blow to him when he learned he would not be playing that year, or ever again, and then finding out about Jeannie was another blow. That had been a tough time for him.

When Don told me Jeannie would be at this meeting, I asked silently, *Lord, is this another one?* I wondered if Don needed to break some ties from his past as well. I mentioned that it was odd how, within one month of each other, someone from our past had come out of the woodwork. He thought I was looking for something that wasn't there. I just prayed silently that if God had an agenda for Don, He would bring it to pass.

I was not able to attend the meeting, but since most of Don's high school buddies were not Christians, I prayed he would have opportunities to share his faith. I encouraged him to be open to what God might want to do, even about Jeannie. I wondered if, deep inside Don's heart, he didn't feel a sense of resentment or betrayal toward her. I prayed that God would allow some dialogue between them if it was needed.

I couldn't believe my attitude. Here was my husband going off to see a former girlfriend and I wasn't in a panic. I trusted Don, and I trusted God's good purpose in his life.

Don came home late that evening, and we talked until 1:30 A.M. Sure enough, God had a plan. Don was able to talk to Jeannie about what had happened, and a cleansing took place. It was not visible to the eye, but God specializes in surgery of the heart.

I continued to pray that God would do His work in our hearts. I did not understand these two encounters, but I knew His Word promises that "His way is perfect," so I rested.

MATT

One week after Don's reunion, I went to our small airport to go to Virginia Beach, Virginia, where I was scheduled to appear on the 700 Club. I was late, so I ran frantically to the ticket counter and checked my luggage. I was told I'd better get to the gate area as the plane was loading. I turned around and nearly ran into Matt, another "tie" from my past. He and I were to be on the same plane. I couldn't believe it. Then I said inside myself, *Lord, You're up to something!*

I had not seen Matt since he and his wife attended my wedding eight years before. I knew about him because of mutual friends, and because he is a popular Christian musician and vocalist. I felt God's Spirit prompting me, so I asked Matt if he'd like for us to sit together to catch up on some of our friends. He said that would be great if we could arrange it. I thought so too, but my feelings were in a turmoil because of the history of our relationship.

In January 1977, I had started attending a church with a friend after not going much for about four years. This church appealed to me because it was filled with people my own age. The pastor was young and had had a dramatic conversion experience, coming out of the drug scene and into a relationship with God. The first time I attended with my friend, we went to a Sunday evening concert. I felt conspicuously new. Then we started attending the Wednesday night Bible study. I liked this because the Bible teaching was interesting as well as practical and challenging.

After a month, my relationship with the Lord began to get back on track. I met new people and enjoyed the fellowship. People were friendly and we started going out for coffee after church.

One evening after the service, I saw a young man walk across the front of the church. Suddenly a startling thought, almost like a voice, flashed across my mind: *That's the guy you're going to marry.*

I thought to myself, *That's weird; I don't even know that guy.* I didn't tell my friend anything about it — I just dismissed those thoughts.

Each time I came to church, the same guy was there. The thought kept coming back: *That's the guy you're going to marry.*

We had just finished studying the life of Gideon, and I remembered how he laid fleeces before the Lord. I wondered if the "voice" I heard was from God or not, so I decided to put out some fleeces. Before church one Wednesday night, I prayed, "If that guy really is the one I'm to marry, let him sit behind me in church." That night he sat behind me.

After two or three months, I said it might be nice if I knew who this guy was. I put out another fleece: "If this really is the guy, then let him introduce himself to me tonight." Matt walked up to me after the service and introduced himself.

During a period of eighteen months, I put out several fleeces, and the results were all positive.

About a year later, I went to one of the pastors and confided in him what was happening. He simply said that if it was the Lord speaking to me, it would come to pass.

In the meantime, I had become friends with Matt and the members of his band, especially a guitar player named Scott. I even went along on several "gigs." Eventually, I shared with Scott what I had been thinking.

Though I never dated Matt once during that time, I felt sure the "voice" I had heard was God. I did not try to manipulate situations, but just kept hoping that if it was God, Matt would be listening. I should say here that there really was no attraction or relationship with Matt other than being friends. I was much closer to Scott than to Matt.

About fifteen months after I'd heard the voice, Matt became engaged. It did not shake me. I found Scripture and substantiation for what I had heard. I walked in faith that it had been God's voice and paid no attention to circumstances. I shared with another musician and his wife about what I had heard, and asked them to pray. I was friends with Matt's fiancée, but I did not share with anyone who I thought would violate the confidence. I believed the voice until the very day I walked into the church for Matt and Becky's wedding. As I sat there, reality sank in. It was not the Lord's voice I had heard so many months before. I was devastated.

I went into a major depression. You see, in the midst of that eighteen months, Don had asked me to marry him and I said no, thinking God had called me to marry Matt. Here I was, twenty-four years old, thinking I had heard God's voice — and I'd been deceived.

The musician whom I had asked to pray called me two days after the wedding and said he and his wife had been fasting and praying. He said as lovingly as he could, "Jan, I've been praying for you, and the Lord showed me through a passage in Ezekiel 13 that you may have heard a lying spirit. That is why it did not come to pass."

A few weeks after the wedding, a mutual friend of Becky's and mine came to me with some distressing news. She had found out that the pastor in whom I had confided nearly a year before had breached my confidence. Not only that, but he also had told Matt and Becky what I thought. They had known for months. I was beside myself with humiliation and embarrassment. I eventually called the pastor and told him how hurt I was. I went to Matt and Becky separately and apologized for any hurt I had caused them. I could barely look at them because of the shame.

Then for the next seven years, I believed another lie: that I could no longer sense God speaking to me. After this whole incident, I felt I had failed God miserably and had made a fool of myself. I also felt God had failed me. How could He have allowed me to believe a lie for all that time? Why didn't He send someone to tell me? I was still committed to the Lord, but I was totally disillusioned.

All of these memories flashed before me as I boarded that plane on my way to the 700 Club. I prayed quickly, "Lord, I know this is no coincidence. What is it you want me to do?"

Matt switched seats and joined me about a half hour into the flight to Dallas. We chatted about all of our mutual friends, families and careers. He was doing a concert in Austin, Texas. I told him about authoring *A Door of Hope* and gave him a copy. I asked about Scott, and Matt showed me pictures of his little boy.

All the while, the Holy Spirit seemed to be speaking to my heart, *Share with him about what happened.*

I was not about to, and I argued silently with the Lord. *I was humiliated once, Lord. Do I have to be humiliated all over again?*

I talked about Don and my girls and how happy we were, but I sensed the Spirit urging me to address the "old business."

I refused.

Tears came to my eyes, and I excused myself and went to the lavatory. Once inside, I said "Lord, please don't make me talk to him about this. The shame and humiliation are unbearable."

The Lord responded simply, *Trust Me, and obey.*

I went back to my seat.

"Matt," I said in a quivering voice, "I need to talk to you. I feel the Lord wants me to share some things with you." I went through the entire story from beginning to end. I could not even look at him, my shame was so great.

At the end, I told him how that incident had devastated my walk with God for nearly seven years and that until a couple of years before, I was totally convinced I could no longer hear God's voice. This was not true any longer, but I had carried the shame far too long.

In his spontaneous, impulsive manner, Matt simply said, "Jan, you were wrong—so what?"

He said several other things, but I heard none of them. Tears filled my eyes and I looked up at him and said, "Matt, thank you. You don't know what that means to me." Those six words wiped away a shroud of humiliation that had enveloped me for years. We parted that day with a hug.

I got onto the next plane, headed for Virginia Beach, and I thanked God for His faithfulness in my life. I thanked Him for orchestrating that meeting, but I still was haunted by one question. "Lord, why didn't You show me I was believing a lie? I am so sorry I listened to a lying spirit. I am so sorry I grieved Your heart."

As clearly as I have ever understood any human's voice, I understood God's whisper: *Jan, I did not see you as believing a lie. I saw your walk of faith. You have the faith of Abraham. I know that when you really do hear My voice, you will obey, no matter what the cost. This, child, is what I saw.* I wept buckets of tears, tears that washed away the residue of shame and embarrassment. From that time until this, I have not doubted being able to hear my Shepherd's voice. Another tie was broken.

DIANE

A week after I returned from Virginia, Don and I were on vacation in Hawaii. I had just completed my master's degree and he wanted us to get away alone to regroup after two long years of school, so he planned this trip as a graduation present for me.

One evening we were listening to a singer in the Royal Hawaiian hotel and enjoying a soft drink. Don went to the restroom, but did not come back for quite awhile. When he returned to the table he had three women with him. One was Diane, a gal whom he had dated in his mid-twenties. He introduced me to all of them and they chatted about all that had happened since they last saw one another. Don had dated Diane before he was a Christian, and I could tell from the conversation that she had liked Don more than he liked her. Walking back to the hotel that night, I said to Don, "That's now two for you, and two for me."

Since he was not that fond of Diane, he again thought I was making something out of what wasn't there. I said, "I think maybe she's never let go and that's why God brought about this meeting." (I still don't know that for sure, but I knew God was doing something in our relationship.)

KATHY

When we got home from our vacation, we talked at length about the events of the summer. I think this was the first time I told him about my prayer. I told him I did not think it was coincidence that we each had encountered two different people from our past, in light of what I had prayed. I ended the conversation with, "Don, God is doing something. I know it. I just want to ask one thing of you. When you hear from Kathy, please do not hide it from me. I would not be able to trust you if you did. When she calls, please let me know."

Don looked at me and shook his head in disbelief. "No way," he said. "She'll never call me."

Three nights later, his friend Larry called. Don answered the phone in the kitchen, and I knew by the conversation who it was. I also knew Larry had maintained friendship with Kathy.

Kathy was Don's girlfriend all through high school and part of college. They had gone together for five years and had talked of marriage. Kathy's family loved Don, and her mother and twin sister even came to our wedding later. At the end of Don's junior year in college, he received a "Dear John" letter from Kathy out of the blue.

All had been fine between him and Kathy, even though he was away at college. They were only a little over an hour apart. He couldn't believe it when he read the letter. Kathy was not only ending their relationship, but she was also marrying someone else in three months. Don tried to call her immediately, but she was at work and had no time to talk. Don felt jilted and rejected. He saw her only one time after that, but he never got over the hurt.

I heard Don say to Larry, "She is? She does? Oh." I had a feeling something was up.

I immediately got up, walked to the kitchen entryway and pointed my finger directly at Don, as if to say, "I told you so."

I was right. Kathy was in town and had called Larry. She wanted to see Don. Larry gave Don her mother's phone number so he could call. He came over to me and said, "What can I say?"

"How about, 'You were right, Jan'?" I said. I knew God had been preparing me for this moment, but I started to feel a little uneasy inside. What if he still loves her? What if she wants him back? What will happen if they see each other after all this time? I wasn't sure.

I sat down with Don and said, "God has ordained this time for you to meet with Kathy. Ask Him what He wants to accomplish." We prayed together and I released him to call her. They made arrangements to meet at her mother's house the next night around 8. I knew this was God's doing—but it still felt a little strange.

Before he left that next night, I took him into my arms and said, "You may need to be honest with her about what you felt. You may need to ask her all the questions you've held inside all these years. Take as long as you need." In caution, I added, "Just remember, I love you and so do our two little girls." We prayed, and with that he was out the door.

The hours went by—9 P.M.; 10; 11; 12—I wished I hadn't told him to take as long as he needed. I continued to pray; I couldn't sleep. Don finally came home just before 2 A.M. He got into bed, and I asked, "How did it go?"

"It was fine," Don said.

"Honey, I don't expect you to tell me all the details, because I respect you and your right to privacy, but I need to know some of what went on. Were you able to share with her at all?" I asked.

Don spent the next hour reviewing their visit. Much of it was with her mother and sister, but Kathy and he did take a walk around the block. Don was able to share his Christian commitment with her, and he found out what had prompted her call. She had recently found several letters he wrote her while in college, and they sparked a lot of hidden emotions. She and her twin sister were adopted and had always known it, but recently she was contacted by her birth mother. This had seemed to bring to the surface a myriad of scenes from her past, of which Don had been a vital part. She wanted to see him.

Don was able to talk to her about his feelings of betrayal and rejection. Both of them cried. They parted that night with a hug. Another tie was broken.

RANDY

That very same night, I called my friend, Lauren.

She was not at home. As I talked to her husband, Randy, I realized this was my final tie. Randy and I had been friends and had dated before he and Lauren became "an item." It was a time in my life when I used men to get things I wanted. I was not proud of that. The Spirit prompted me to talk to Randy and ask for his forgiveness. Although the four of us had been close friends for almost fifteen years, these issues had never been addressed directly. I told Randy I was sorry. He thanked me, and I hung up the phone – free.

My ties to the past were broken.

Breaking Unhealthy Emotional Ties

I have gone into lengthy detail about these events to show you how they were authored by God for a purpose beyond what I know. I am certain He used them to answer the prayer of a wife whose heart longed for deeper unity with her husband. In a way that I cannot fully explain, God reached into the depths of our emotional and spiritual realms to break ties that were preventing unity.

I am NOT recommending you plan such events.

I am NOT recommending you contact former boy-friends or girlfriends to resolve old relationships.

I AM recommending that, if you desire unity in your marriage, you begin to pray and ask God to show you the obstacles.

I AM recommending that, if you are aware of some unhealthy emotional ties to someone other than your mate, you ask God to break those ties. This may mean that you sit down with the Lord and confess any fantasies, or preoc-cupation of thought about that person, or that you express feelings and emotions still tied up with that person. Ask God to sever all those ties and to redirect all the emotions and preoccupations into a richer, healthier love for your mate.

Stumbling block #2: Unyielding control

A second area that may be a stumbling block to building unity in your marriage is unyielding control of certain areas of your life. When victims marry, control is a big issue. Most victims of dysfunctional homes struggle with a need for control. When control is lost, the victims often panic or make desperate attempts to regain control.

Think about it for a moment: A little girl grows up in a home where she is sexually abused. She does not know when it will happen, how often it will occur, or what would happen to her if someone found out. She feels helpless and powerless over her situation. She often makes an inner vow never to be that vulnerable again.

A little boy grows up with a dad who is seldom there. When his dad is there, he is distant, critical and unloving. He makes promises and does not come through. The boy's mother says nothing about the father's drinking problem or any other problem for that matter. The little boy grows up believing that if he can achieve enough, someone may pay attention to him. He feels frightened because life seems so unpredictable. As an adult, he is afraid of change, and he becomes emotionally cut-off and rigid in an attempt to ward off the intense emotions bubbling below the surface. This is what it is like for victims.

Now imagine that these two marry each other. Can you see the fireworks?

Don and I have had to learn through the last ten years or so to yield certain areas of control. When we are unwilling to yield in certain areas in a relationship, chances are those are problem areas. Even when you both yield, you may experience conflict.

One key in knowing if you are unyielding is whether or not you use deception to maintain control. Probably the area in which it has been the toughest for me to yield has been money. When I work, I want the right to spend *MY* money, but early in our marriage, God nailed me. He showed me that this area was out of balance, that I was keeping secrets from Don, and that I was not wanting to yield to Don's direction in the area of finances.

I would go out and buy things and then put them into my closet and leave them there for weeks before I'd get them out to wear.

When Don would ask, "Honey, is that a new dress?" I would say, "Oh, no, I've had it for weeks." (I know a number of other women who can relate to this.)

The Lord put His finger on this area one day and said to me, *This is deception. Stop it!*

It was so hard for me, but I did.

When Don asked me why I didn't just tell him the truth, all I could say was I thought I would get into trouble. It came from my background but it was not honoring God, and deception always creates division.

Are there areas in your life in which you are unwilling to yield control? As you examine these areas, ask God to help you develop the trust needed to yield according to His will.

Stumbling block #3: Unforgiving attitudes

The last stumbling block to unity is an unforgiving attitude. If you've been married any length of time, you probably can recall a time or two when your mate has let you down. When we carry unforgiveness toward our mate, it prevents our building on fresh soil. It is like building on an old foundation that does not suit the house we're trying to put up. The structure is destined to fall.

I know of one couple, both of them victims, who each has an ongoing record of all the offenses committed against that person by the mate. The trouble is, even when one of them tries to change some behavior, the other discounts it as insignificant compared to the list of offenses. I call this "box mentality" or "keeping a file" on your mate.

If you are one who puts your mate into a box, that is, predetermines how he will respond in a given situation, then you will find it to be a predictable, but confining relationship. "Keeping a file" is similar to that, yet it is different in that it contains evidence. Every unkind thing your mate has ever said is in that file, and you pull it out when you think you need it. I know, because I used to be an excellent file-keeper on Don. Any time we had a conflict, I could recite several other instances to prove my point. I am still too good at this, but I have tried in the last several years to burn my files. When any of us keeps a file on our mate, it keeps us all from growing.

We have talked about three distinctive stumbling blocks to unity: (1) unbroken ties from the past, (2) unyielding areas of control, and (3) unforgiving attitudes. Take time to look in your own file right now.

- Do you have ties that need to be broken?
- Are there areas where you have been obstinate and need to be more willing to compromise?
- Are you confining your mate to a "box" or "keeping a file" of evidence just in case you need it when the next conflict arises?

If so, these stumbling blocks need to be removed. Ask the Lord to give you a willing heart to yield to Him first in these areas; then get a wheelbarrow, cart the blocks away, and go on to dwell in unity.

13

Dwelling in Unity

Dwelling in unity — most of us want that. We miss it when it is absent, yet we rarely appreciate it when we do have it.

I recently had a five-day speaking engagement in Wisconsin. With small children, it is difficult to be away for that length of time, so I try to limit the number of those kinds of engagements. When I do accept one, I try to think ahead about meals, lunches and groceries so I can purchase needed items before I leave. Although Don has been "Mr. Mom" successfully on several occasions, it is important to me to do as much as I can to make the time I am away easier for him.

Last Tuesday was no different. My flight to Wisconsin was scheduled for early departure Wednesday morning, so I was to spend the night with my friend, Ginny, who would take me to the airport. I had spent the day grocery shopping, doing laundry and getting the house in order. I made a nice dinner that evening, knowing my family would be without Mom's cooking for a while. After doing the dishes, I put some blueberry muffins in the oven, and went off to pack my clothes and materials.

Don, who is an avid Chicago Cubs fan, sat in the

living room watching a game. Time ticked away and pressure began building in me. When the girls came into my room and asked me to do something, I told them Mommie was busy and to go find Dad. I knew that by this time, the Cub game was over. The girls came back; they couldn't find Dad. I became irritated. *Where is Don when I need him? He should know I'm under a lot of pressure. It's like always—I have to carry the whole load.*

Suddenly, Kellie yelled, "Mom, it smells like something is burning." I ran to the kitchen and pulled the charred blueberry muffins out of the oven. Angry at myself, I still wondered where Don was. I went back to packing.

In the meantime, Don showed up and got the girls ready for bed, and I asked if he could pack a box of my tapes for me. He did. When I was finally ready, I carried my luggage to the dining room. Again, Don was not around, so I loaded the things into the car, saying to myself, *He should know I need help.*

I said good-bye to the girls, promising I would bring them a surprise. Don now appeared in the kitchen, packing his lunch for the next day. I said, "Well, I'm ready to go."

The tension between us was obvious. We were not in unity—we were in a strained state of discord.

"I don't like you to leave when things are like this," Don said.

"I don't like it either. Can we go sit down in the living room?" I asked.

We sat on the couch and I explained how I was feeling. I told Don I felt a lot of pressure when I was to be gone so long and I was trying hard to do things that would make it easier on him.

At first he said, "Jan, sometimes I think you try too hard. Why don't you just leave? We'll be fine, you know. It's not like I haven't done this before."

We talked a bit more, and I realized that what really bothered me was that I would miss Don, and in the midst of packing, my anger masked my true feelings. I really wanted him to come and be close to me while I got ready, and I became frustrated when he was nowhere to be found.

As I shared this with Don, he realized something else, too. He said, "I guess I deal with your leaving by avoiding you. I was outside fixing a sprinkler while you were packing. I really didn't need to do it then, but I guess I just didn't want to face your being gone so long."

As we talked, I realized I needed to take responsibility for my part of the current predicament. I said, "Honey, I'm really sorry. I should have listened to what I was feeling inside. I should have gone to find you and asked you to come and be with me. Instead, I went into being angry and expecting you to know. This is my old pattern of dealing with feelings of abandonment by masking them with anger."

Don said, "I need to appreciate you more, too. Sometimes I don't tell you how thankful I am for all you do. I also need to recognize when I'm avoiding an unpleasant situation by withdrawing. I think I deal with my feelings of abandonment by running away."

We sat on the couch, hugged, and prayed together, committing to each other that we would try to be aware of our individual responsibilities in future situations. Unity was restored.

I could have left that night in a huff, but we chose to resolve the immediate circumstances. I believe couples get into trouble when they allow these incidents to go unaddressed. Unfortunately, these minor altercations have a way of building up over time, then exploding. That is why I believe the Scripture admonishes us: "Be angry, and do not sin; do not let the sun go down on your wrath, nor give place to the devil" (Ephesians 4:26,27). We may not always be able to resolve conflicts quickly, but they do need to be addressed and talked over. Unity can be restored even if the situation at hand has not been totally resolved.

ACHIEVING UNITY

Achieving unity in a marriage takes work. We started our building project by basing it on the foundation of God's Word in Proverbs 24:3,4. The Amplified Version is especially poignant:

> Through skillful and godly Wisdom is a house [a life, a home, a family] built, and by understanding it is established [on a sound and good foundation]. And by knowledge shall the chambers [of its every area] be filled with all precious and pleasant riches.

What a description of unity!

What key ingredients did you note as you read that verse? Chuck Swindoll elaborates on them:

> Wisdom: Seeing with discernment. It's having a broad perspective. The term stresses accuracy, the ability to sense that which is beneath the surface . . .
>
> Understanding: Responding with insight. Establishing your marriage calls for this ingredient. As I view something with discernment (from God's perspective), I am better equipped to respond with insight, not to take it personally or feel the need to fight back.
>
> Knowledge: Learning with perception. It includes having a teachable spirit, a willingness to hear, a desire to discover. Knowledge includes taking the time and going to the trouble to learn. Growing, healthy mates are in constant pursuit of the truth.[1]

As I reflected on dwelling in unity in marriage, I thought about some practical ways we can reinforce the stability of our union. When victims marry, they need an additional measure of the "reinforcing steel bars" that secure the foundation to the structure of the home.

"Re-bar" #1 – **U**nderstanding

"Re-bar" #2 – **N**ourishing

"Re-bar" #3 – **I**ntercession

"Re-bar" #4 – **T**rust

"Re-bar" #5 – **Y**ourself

UNDERSTANDING

Understanding is a vital ingredient for those who come from dysfunctional backgrounds. Webster's dictionary says understanding is "to be thoroughly familiar with the character and propensities of something or someone; to show a sympathetic or tolerant attitude toward."

Don and I have had to develop understanding for each other, not only with regard to our background issues, but also the differences in our temperaments, likes and dislikes, and our motivating passions. Sometimes it is hard for me to understand how Don can get so involved in a ball game, but I have grown to appreciate his intensity and his integrity. I may never share the exact same passion for the Cubs that Don has, or feel the frustration he does when his basketball team doesn't play up to their ability, but I understand and am compassionate toward him in these situations.

Don may never fully grasp the betrayal I experienced as a child, but he has come to understand the ramifications of the injury I suffered. He has consistently shown an attitude of loving understanding which has enabled us to go beyond the past and build a solid relationship for both ourselves and our family.

NOURISHING

In the Scripture, the words *nurturing* and *nourishing* are closely related. Ephesians 5:29 says: "No one ever hated his own flesh, but nourishes and cherishes it, just as the Lord does the church." Nourishing means promoting the growth of something by providing the substances needed.

We usually think of this term in connection with our children rather than our mates. Yet when we grow up in dysfunctional homes, we oftentimes have lacked proper nurturing. There is a healthy nourishing that can go on in a marital relationship, but there is a counterfeit as well.

John Bradshaw states:

> Two half-people create an entrapment or enmeshment, rather than a relationship . . . Each is entrapped by needing the other for completion. As the years roll on and the fear of going it alone increases, each becomes more and more trapped . . . They are held together in an emotional symbiosis . . . They become bonded by their neediness.

Bradshaw continues,

> In a healthy relationship, each person is bonded by desire and not out of neediness. Therefore, each is in the process of becoming more or less whole. Two whole people who guard each other's wholeness come together and grow because of the guardianship of the other.[2]

Nourishing in a healthy manner means we can provide for our mate an environment of encouragement and enthusiasm that will promote his or her growth. On a practical level, I try to be sensitive to some of Don's deeper, unspoken needs.

Last night, I noticed that he went to bed while I was on the phone. He seemed somewhat preoccupied at dinner but we had no time to "connect" before a prayer meeting that I had at our house. After ending my phone conversation, I sensed that Don needed some encouragement. When I walked into our bedroom, he was lying on the bed, looking at the ceiling. I said, "I just came to give you some hugs."

As we lay there, he shared the events of his day that had troubled him. I held him close and simply listened. When I got up to leave, he said, "Thanks for coming in to be with me. I've missed you. It seems like we haven't had a lot of time together in the last few days."

Just that simple act reconnected us and brought more unity.

INTERCESSION

How often do you spend prayer time interceding for your mate? Intercession is a prayer, petition or entreaty in behalf of another.

Sometimes we are so busy praying for others we forget to include our mate. We often pray from crisis to crisis, rather than going before God's throne daily for our mate.

I have several women friends who share a similar heart's desire regarding their mates. We have covenanted together to pray consistently for our husbands. We have not disclosed the nature of our prayer to anyone outside our group, but we get together on a regular basis to share how God has been faithful to answer those prayers. It has been exciting to see the results, but this also has been a wonderful means of drawing our hearts into a deeper union with our mates.

"Confess your trespasses to one another, and pray for one another, that you may be healed. The effective, fervent prayer of a righteous man avails much" (James 5:16). We are promised that persistent prayer works!

Another wonderful promise in Scripture is contained in Job 22:21-30 (AMP). The beginning of the passage says, "Acquaint now yourself with Him [agree with God and show yourself to be conformed to His will] and be at peace; by that [you shall prosper and great] good shall come to you."

The final promise in verse 30 is this: "He will even deliver the one [for whom you intercede] who is not innocent; yes, he will be delivered through the cleanness of your hands." This is the power of intercession, when we are rightly related to our God.

TRUST

The ability to trust has been deeply fractured in the lives of many who have grown up in dysfunctional backgrounds. When victims marry, each mate must make an investment in building trust in the relationship.

How is trust built? Don already addressed some specific ways that husbands can help to build trust in his chapter, "Is the Roof Leaking?" Let me share some basic principles in building trust.

Truth is a vital component. We must have the confidence that our mate is honest and can be believed before trust will develop.

Credibility is another element. Consistency and credibility of word and action must be present if we are to trust one another.

Sensitivity or compassion is needed if we are to develop a deep level of trust. We can be vulnerable only with those in whom we feel a sense of safety and understanding. We learn to trust a person who will not violate our confidence or who does not regard lightly the details of something we regard as meaningful.

Trust means "assured reliance on the character, ability, strength or truth of someone." As we indicated earlier, trust takes time to build, and it ultimately must rest in our trust in God. If we are unable to trust God, it will be difficult to trust our mate. Why? Because God is the only one who is perfectly trustworthy. If we cannot trust the one who is always faithful, we will have an arduous task in trusting our mate who, at times, will let us down. As we learn to trust God, we will be better able to trust our mate and establish greater unity.

YOURSELF

It might seem obvious to some that you must make an investment of yourself, if unity is to be characteristic of your marital relationship. Unfortunately, in our society we have not fully grasped what it means actually to invest of ourselves. Many men believe that providing a lovely home, a big bank account and a vacation home at the beach is what investing in their families means. Many women believe that if they stay home, provide balanced meals and home-school their children, this is enough. There is absolutely nothing wrong with these things — unless they become substitutes for giving of oneself.

What exactly does that mean? Some of the most intimate experiences Don and I share take place when we reveal our dreams, feelings, disappointments and innermost thoughts to each other. As we come out from behind our walls of protection and allow our mates to glimpse what really matters in our hearts, we are giving of ourselves.

Recently Don and I had a conversation about his boyhood. We ended by praying about some of the things he felt he missed. As he openly expressed to the Lord his desire to have God meet some of his innermost needs, I was deeply touched. Our time together was one of the most intimate times we have ever shared. I think Don would say the same.

Giving of ourselves is one sure way to secure unity. It is important to note that the previous four elements will probably have to be present before we can share ourselves comfortably. We have a wonderful role model to follow.

> Let each of you look out not only for his own interests, but also for the interest of others. Let this mind be in you which was also in Christ Jesus, who, being in the form of God, did not consider it robbery to be equal with God, but made Himself of no reputation, taking the form of a servant, and coming in the likeness of men (Philippians 2:4-7).

Jesus chose to divest Himself of all that was rightly His to secure unity with God for us. So must we give of ourselves in relationship with our mates, that by our love others will know we are His.

FINAL INSPECTION

We have come to the final inspection of our construction project. We have seen the importance of discovering the cracks in our individual foundations and in obtaining a soil report to reveal the content of our family backgrounds. We have secured the finest Architect and Master Builder to complete the project. He has provided us with a detailed blueprint to follow that insures structural soundness.

We have found that periodic inspections are necessary and that plumbing difficulties are inevitable, but not beyond repair. We have provided a "critical path method" to help you pour a new foundation in your marriage. We have outlined the framing of the house and distinguished between walls of support and walls of division and between healthy insulation and unhealthy isolation. Don has shared about some possible attitude leaks in the roof and how those leaks can be patched. We have presented you with a homeowners' insurance plan that will prevent unexpected "critters in the attic" and have brought to light some common stumbling blocks to unity. Finally, we have introduced five essential ingredients for dwelling together in unity.

We have shared with you some of the common pitfalls that occur when victims marry. We pray that you have been encouraged and that you will seek the Master Builder for His direction regarding your "house." We are absolutely convinced that God is able to restore relationships and that He desires to do so. As we yield ourselves to Him, allowing Him free reign to repair the "waste places" in our lives, we are no longer victims, but *victors* in Him! "Thanks be to God, who gives us the victory through our Lord Jesus Christ" (1 Corinthians 15:51).

As we come together in unity in our Lord, He promises to "build the house," and assures us that every house that is established on the Rock will stand firm. Unite your hearts in Him. He is the only sure Foundation.

We leave you with a beautiful description of the

marital unity that is available only in Him. May it bless you, inspire you and bond you together in Him.

Sorrow and Joy

As sorrowful, yet always rejoicing (2 Corinthians 6:10).

Sorrow was beautiful, but her beauty was the beauty of the moonlight shining through the leafy branches of the trees in the wood, and making little pools of silver here and there on the soft green moss below.

When Sorrow sang, her notes were like the low, sweet call of the nightingale, and in her eyes was the unexpectant gaze of one who has ceased to look for coming gladness. She could weep in tender sympathy with those who weep, but to rejoice with those who rejoice was unknown to her.

Joy was beautiful, too, but his was the radiant beauty of the summer morning. His eyes still held the glad laughter of childhood, and his hair had the glint of the sunshine's kiss. When Joy sang his voice soared upward as the lark's, and his step was the step of a conqueror who has never known defeat. He could rejoice with all who rejoice, but to weep with those who weep was unknown to him.

"We can never be united," said Sorrow wistfully.

"No, never." And Joy's eyes shadowed as he spoke. "My path lies through the sunlit meadows; the sweetest roses bloom for my gathering, and the blackbirds and thrushes await my coming to pour forth their most joyous lays.

"My path," said Sorrow, turning slowly away, "leads through the darkening woods; with moon-flowers only shall my hands be filled. Yet the sweetest of all earth songs—the love song of the night—shall be mine; farewell, Joy, farewell."

Even as she spoke they became conscious of a form standing beside them, dimly seen, but of a Kingly

Presence, and a great and holy awe stole over them as they sank on their knees before Him.

"I see Him as the King of Joy," whispered Sorrow, "for on His Head are many crowns, and the nailprints in His hands and feet are the scars of a great victory. Before Him all my sorrow is melting away into deathless love and gladness, and I give myself to Him forever."

"Nay, Sorrow," said Joy softly, "but I see Him as the King of Sorrow, and the crown on His head is a crown of thorns, and the nailprints in His hands and feet are the scars of a great agony. I, too, give myself to Him forever, for sorrow with Him must be sweeter than any joy I have known."

"Then we are one in Him," they cried in gladness, "for none but He could unite Joy and Sorrow."

Hand in hand they passed out into the world to follow Him through storm and sunshine, in the bleakness of winter cold and the warmth of summer gladness, "as sorrowful yet always rejoicing."[3]

He has been faithful in our lives to "redeem" the sorrows. He has restored to us, in His great love, all that we have lacked, and He has rebuilt our relationship on a solid foundation.

Whoever comes to Me, and hears My sayings and does them, I will show you whom he is like: He is like a man building a house, who dug deep and laid the foundation on the rock. And when the flood arose, the stream beat vehemently against that house, and could not shake it, for it was founded on the rock (Luke 6:47,48).

He wants to do that for you!

Get your tools in hand, lay your foundation in Him — and build on.

Reference Notes

Chapter 1b – Faulty Foundations – Don

1. Claudia Black, *It Will Never Happen to Me*, (New York: Ballantine Books, 1981), pp. 24-38.
2. Adapted from *Home Away From Home* by Janet Woititz (Pompano Beach, FL: Health Communications, Inc., 1987), pp. 69-80.

Chapter 2 – Preparing the Soil

1. Charles Swindoll, *Strike the Original Match* (Portland, OR: Multnomah Press, 1980), p. 21.

Chapter 3 – Who Needs an Architect? Or Blueprints?

1. Charles Swindoll, *Strike the Original Match* (Portland, OR: Multnomah Press, 1980), p. 31.

Chapter 6 – Repairing the Foundation

1. David Seamands, *Healing of Memories* (Wheaton, IL: Victor Books, 1985), p. 34.
2. Gordon Dalbey, *Healing the Masculine Soul* (Waco, TX: Word Books, 1988).
3. Jan Frank, *A Door of Hope* (San Bernardino, CA: Here's Life Publishers, 1987), pp. 107-129.
4. Oswald Chambers, *My Utmost for His Highest* (New York: Dodd, Mead & Company, 1963), p. 243.

Chapter 7 – Framing the House

1. Charles Swindoll, *Strike the Original Match* (Portland, OR: Multnomah Press, 1980), p. 159.

Chapter 8 – Walls of Support/Walls of Division

1. Harriet Lerner, *The Dance of Anger* (New York: Perennial Library, Harper & Row, 1985), p. 57.
2. Clifford and Joyce Penner, *The Gift of Sex* (Waco, TX: Word Books, 1981), p. 209.

Chapter 9 – Insulation vs. Isolation

1. Lois Mowday, *The Snare* (Colorado Springs, CO: Nav Press, 1988), pp. 48-49.

Chapter 10 – Is the Roof Leaking? – Don

1. David Seamands, *Healing of Memories* (Wheaton, IL: Victor Books, 1985), p. 163.
2. Jan Silvious, *Please Don't Say You Need Me* (Grand Rapids, MI: Zondervan Publishing House, 1989), p. 24.

Chapter 13 – Dwelling in Unity

1. Charles Swindoll, *Strike the Original Match* (Portland, OR: Multnomah Press, 1980), p. 24.
2. John Bradshaw, *Bradshaw on: The Family* (Deerfield Beach, FL: Health Communications Inc., 1988), p. 65.
3. Mrs. Charles E. Cowman, *Streams in the Desert*, Vol. 1 (Grand Rapids: Zondervan Publishing House, 1965, revised from original 1925 edition), pp. 243-44.

Recommended Reading List

Christian books:

Bateman, Lana. *God's Crippled Children*. Dallas: Philippian Ministries, 1981, 1985. (Obtainable from: Philippian Ministries, 8515 Greenville Ave., Suite #103, Dallas, TX 75243.)

Buhler, Rich. *Pain and Pretending*. Nashville, TN: Thomas Nelson Publishers, 1988.

Frank, Jan. *A Door of Hope*. San Bernardino, CA: Here's Life Publishers, 1987.

Hancock, Maxine, and Maines, Karen. *Child Sexual Abuse.* Wheaton, IL: Harold Shaw Publishers, 1987.

Littauer, Fred and Florence. *Freeing Your Mind From Memories That Bind.* San Bernardino, CA: Here's Life Publishers, 1988.

(**NOTE:** It is best to use this book in conjunction with individual counseling as working through the book may evoke distressing emotions or repressed memories that require professional assistance to deal with.)

Marriage books:

Barnes, Bob and Emilie. *Growing a Great Marriage.* Eugene, OR: Harvest House Publishers, 1988.

Congo, Dr. David and Jan. *Free to Soar.* Old Tappan, NJ: Fleming H. Revell, 1987.

McDowell, Josh. *The Secret of Loving.* San Bernardino, CA: Here's Life Publishers, 1985.

Smalley, Gary, and Trent, John, Ph.D. *The Language of Love.* Pomona, CA: Focus on the Family Publishers, 1988.

Wright, Norm. *Communication: Key to Your Marriage.* Ventura, CA: Regal Books, 1979.

Secular books:

Bradshaw, John. *Bradshaw on: The Family.* Deerfield Beach, FL: Health Communications, Inc., 1988.

Carnes, Peter. *Out of the Shadows.* Minneapolis, MN: CompCare Publishers, 1983.

Lerner, Harriet, Ph.D. *The Dance of Anger.* New York: Perennial Library, Harper & Row, 1985.

ACA books:

Black, Claudia. *It Will Never Happen to Me.* New York: Ballantine Books, 1981.

Kritsberg, Wayne. *The Adult Children of Alcoholics Syndrome.* Deerfield Beach, FL: Health Communications, Inc., 1985.

Seixas, Judith S. and Youch, Geraldine. *Children of Alcoholism: A Survival Manual.* New York: Perennial Library, 1985.

Woititz, Janet. *Home Away From Home.* Pompano Beach, FL: Health Communications, Inc., 1987.

More help for those who have been victims.

Quantity		Total
____	**A DOOR OF HOPE** by Jan Frank. The national bestseller that enables you to recognize and resolve the pains of an abusive childhood through 10 effective steps for healing. 0-89840-187-9/$7.95	$_____
____	**A DOOR OF HOPE (AUDIO TAPE)** by Jan Frank. The helpful audio tape presentation based on the bestselling book. (One tape) 0-89840-266-2/$7.95	$_____
____	**ARE YOU A VICTIM OF YOUR WIFE'S PAST?** by Don Frank. As the husband of Jan Frank, Don shares how husbands can empathize with their wives, encourage them, and help them resolve painful childhood memories. (One tape) 0-89840-261-1/$7.95	$_____
____	**FREEING YOUR MIND FROM MEMORIES THAT BIND** by Fred and Florence Littauer. For those who have suffered emotional trauma such as emotional, physical or sexual abuse: How to find freedom from the hurts of the past. 0-89840-232-8/$8.95	$_____

Order Total $_____

Indicate product(s) desired above. Fill out below.
Send to:

HERE'S LIFE PUBLISHERS, INC.
P. O. Box 1576
San Bernardino, CA 92402-1576

NAME_____

ADDRESS_____

STATE_____ZIP_____

☐ Payment (check or money order only)
  included
☐ Visa   ☐ Mastercard #_____

Expiration Date_____Signature_____

**FOR FASTER SERVICE
CALL TOLL FREE:
1-800-950-4457**

ORDER TOTAL $_____

SHIPPING and
HANDLING $_____
($1.50 for one book,
$0.50 for each additional.
Do not exceed $4.00.)

APPLICABLE
SALES TAX (CA, 6%) $_____

TOTAL DUE $_____

PAYABLE IN U.S. FUNDS.
(No cash orders accepted.)

WVM 274-3

Your Christian bookstore should have these in stock. If not, use this "Shop-by-Mail" form.
PLEASE ALLOW 2 TO 4 WEEKS FOR DELIVERY.
PRICES SUBJECT TO CHANGE WITHOUT NOTICE.